THE CANNABIBLE 3

texada timewarp

THE CANNABIBLE 3

JASON KING

TEN SPEED PRESS

Berkeley

This book is dedicated to the online communities at
overgrow.com and cannabisworld.com without which
this book would be much less than it is. Thank you!

Many mahalos to: DJ Short, Chimera, Jorge Cervantes, Annie Nelson, Toni Tajima, Jasmine Star, John Lee Pedimore, Mr. Dank, *Cannabis Culture* magazine, HeadVripper, Reeferman, Meadow, Jeremiah, SeaWeed, Happy, Nc & C, Legends Seeds, MCU, Bubbleman, 420times, Mila Jansen, THSeeds, DNA Genetics, Dr. Atomic, Big I Brian, Breeder Steve, Shabud, Don, Shroomy420, The Massachusetts Chemdawg Family, Grady, VisionCreator, Chris Iverson, Beltoforion, MarkSurfs, ShantiBaba, and B Rad.

All rights reserved. Published in the United States by Ten Speed Press, an imprint of the Crown Publishing Group, a division of Random House, Inc., New York.
www.crownpublishing.com
www.tenspeed.com

Ten Speed Press and the Ten Speed Press colophon are registered trademarks of Random House, Inc.

Library of Congress Cataloging-in-Publication Data on file with the publisher.

ISBN: 978-1-58008-784-1

Printed in China

Book design by Toni Tajima
Project management by Annie Nelson
Copyediting by Jasmine Star
Proofreading by Kim Catanzarite

13 12 11 10 9 8 7 6 5 4

First edition

CONTENTS

INTRODUCTION TO THE FOREWORD

by DJ Short

When Jason King asked me if I would like to write a foreword to *The Cannabible 3*, I was honored and excited to do so. There were many things I wanted to cover, primarily about the cannabis community's actualization as both a culture and a community. I began an outline of relevant topics and quickly became overwhelmed by the project. In all honesty, I found myself time and again seeking assistance from an old friend, mentor, and alter ego, Mr. Lee Stanley Danielski.

Mr. D. and I go way back, sharing similar views about most situations, and it is his opinion and input I value most regarding social, political, and philosophical issues. I found myself continually returning to Mr. D. for advice and counsel on the project. Finally, I simply asked if he would be willing to accept the challenge of writing this forward, and he said yes.

I owe a debt of gratitude to Mr. D. and would like to say thank you and that I greatly appreciate your help and support. Here's to a long and fruitful relationship. Although this piece is specifically about our cannabis community, it also addresses many aspects of the broader cooperative community, and indeed it is necessary to digress from the topic of cannabis to do so. Please realize the need to focus on these broader issues as a means to our overall success and acceptance. As a balance, I'd like to begin with a few words concerning what I feel is truly good herb.

WHAT IS GOOD HERB?

Good herb, for me, primarily provides a feeling of enjoyment, well-being, and creative stimulation. Good herb also opens up my mind and heart to possibilities I otherwise may have overlooked. Good herb counters many of the day-to-day distractions that clutter my being by providing deeper insights and alternative ways of being and thinking. Perhaps among the worst of these day-to-day distractions are the urges to compete, conquer, and control, those my masculine conditioning imposes upon me. With good herb, I am better able to experience my Buddha nature and the holistic wellness the subtleties of the feminine mystique offer.

Perhaps this is one of the reasons we all enjoy the female cannabis plants the most. At any rate, good herb allows me to better experience the possibilities of my totality as opposed to merely my conditioning. Good herb increases my desire to act cooperatively toward the betterment of the world for all. It definitely inspires a greater sense of passive creativity.

Potency, in and of itself, is not necessarily an aspect of quality. Potency is, however, an aspect of quantity. A comparison in the wine and spirits industry would be between a fine, aged whiskey and pure grain alcohol, or between a fine Merlot and a fortified wine. In both cases, the first is a high-quality, handcrafted specialty libation, while the second offers the most bang for the buck. For me, potency is far less important than the quality of the effect a certain variety creates. In fact, some of the overly potent products are quite the opposite of an enjoyable experience.

Good herb helps me to better think, dream, meditate, and be. It adds color, flavor, and richness to an already extraordinary world. It inspires a healthy excitement about the experience of life, along with consolation for pain and anxiety. Good herb helps increase my sense of tolerance toward diversity as well. It brightens my day and puts a smile on my face and a spring in my step, or it makes me dreamy, relaxed, and composed. It is either contemplative or creative, motivational or relaxing. Good herb can often bring up old memories associated with unique smells and tastes.

One of the things I most enjoy about truly good herb is the sense of flow it can induce. It's often motivational, and I find myself doing chores or working on projects without thinking much about it until I am deeply immersed in the flow. Things get done, life gets organized, chaos becomes clear—signs of truly good herb.

Occasionally, truly good herb is also capable of being quite subtle. Sometimes the truly good herb experience is not fully recognized until hours after consumption when one finds oneself immersed in a focused project or deep in the outback of an enhanced imagination. This effect is easily verifiable with simple re-examination of product. Personally, and more so as I age, I prefer the effects of the subtle-but-lasting good herb experience.

My standards for what qualifies as truly good herb, compared to what qualifies as pretty good herb, are very high indeed. It is important to note that as one samples better and better herb, the best becomes the standard by which to judge. Luckily for me, among the best are Highland Gold Oaxacan, Colombian (Santa Marta), Guerrero Green, Acapulco Gold, certain island herbs such as Hawaiian, Maui Wowie, and Kona Gold, and the mind-altering Thais, to name a few. Due to my fondness for these pinnacles of cannabis quality, coupled with all of the great hashish I've had the good fortune to have sampled, my standards are quite high.

There is a lot of pretty good herb out there. Some of it is almost equal in desirability to truly good herb but not quite. It usually lacks some specific trait or nuance found only in the complex and complete makeup of truly good herb. Lately, the truly good herb experience for me has been in the form of hashish, resin, or oil. But sometimes, albeit only rarely and during an exceptional season, it is from something that I produce outdoors. Nowadays, truly good herb on any commercial level is very rare (except in the form of professionally produced, cured, and packaged hashish). In my experience, truly good herb comes only from environmental "sweet spots," such as the Oaxaca highlands, Colombia, Thailand, Hawaii, and Nepal, where it has been allowed to acclimate to landrace status. It has not been commercially available for quite some time, but small boutique backyard gardens are sometimes capable of producing noteworthy samples. Once again, properly produced and cured hashish and cannabis resin are another story.

From a baseline state, the experience of good herb begins with a sensation of flavor after the first hit. I savor the essence, which ranges in palate, as it melds with my being like the perfect harmony of a familiar song. An immediate flush of old memories are usually inspired by the initial taste, often in a jumbled cacophony. I sometimes encounter a unique essence that I can only refer to as "ethnic holiday" because it reminds me of the mix of flavors and odors that I remember from holiday family gatherings I attended as a young child. Smells and tastes of ethnic food (Polish and other eastern European delights for me) coupled with various perfumes, colognes, tobacco, coffee, pine, and cedar and floral undertones with a hint of church incense or a scented candle blend with the memories of good and happy times. Good herb often evokes these fond memories, usually accompanied during the initial rush by the experience of that familiar and welcomed "warm and fuzzy hug from within" (thank you A.H.).

Giddiness is another desirable state offered by truly good herb. That playful sense of fun innate to many creatures is often stimulated by truly good herb, initiating a fun quest. When a trait such as inspired giddiness is associated with a good herb, it is also usually very consistent in its effect, not only over time but also between individuals.

There is usually little or no tolerance effect associated with truly good herb. That is, truly good herb is always truly good herb for anyone who experiences it, every time and anytime. One never becomes burnt-out on truly good herb, it merely runs out, and often too soon!

The multijar test is perhaps the best test for good herb. When testing several varieties of herb, the one that runs out first is often the best, especially if a group has access to the stash.

The existence of truly good herb is indeed symbiotic with those who share its compassionate nature. It teaches compassion on an operative level. Perhaps truly good herb could qualify as an "entactogen," the term given to empathy-inducing drugs, such as MDMA. It tends to resensitize one to the need and suffering in the world that is often so overwhelming and overlooked. It inspires a sense of concern and commitment to address and alleviate such need and suffering as well.

I could explore many specific traits concerning the aspects of truly good herb: flavor, palate, head and body feelings, symptomatic signs, and so on. But for now, perhaps the point I wish to stress most is that truly good herb is indeed special and deserves recognition and appreciation for this simple fact, and hopefully a grand resurrection someday soon.

FOREWORD: CANNABIS AND COMMUNITY

by Lee Stanley Danielski
with DJ Short

All are offered a path. All have the free choice to decide the direction of their own path. Every choice one makes, every decision and action, determines one's direction. Those who share a similar direction are apt to notice one another. Those who recognize the similarity shared, and who cooperate toward success for all, are a community. The communities I choose to belong to are characterized by cooperation and responsible participation as opposed to social control, competition, and domination. People in cooperative communities share the common dream of autonomy via self-actualization and responsible self-sufficiency. We seek to establish a sustainable, independent, responsible self-sufficiency for all who choose this path.

CONTROL VERSUS SELF-DETERMINATION

Unfortunately, those who choose to peacefully cooperate are often systematically usurped and exploited by the legions invested in social and personal control via misinformation, fear, and violence. It's obvious to anyone paying attention that our current systems of governance are corrupt to the core—scams perpetrated for millennia by unscrupulous hacks and their willing toadies—and we're conditioned to consider them the norm.

A grand and imaginative enlightenment is required to break the chains that bind us to this predicament. Our cooperative communities have been at the forefront of such an awakening for a while. Through art, literature, music, science, craft and trade, gardening and farming, meditation, and deep inner and social insight, we have accumulated a vast network of relevant information—enough to render any ruling elite moot and useless. Our goal is ultimately to establish a foundation upon which to nourish a safe haven for the creative, imaginative, and responsible entre-preneur, who in turn will provide a safe haven for the passive, the infirm, and the meek.

The primary obstacle to our goal is and has been the over-bearing control of some form of tyranny, including fascism. And the antidote to oppressive, tyrannical fascism and ultracontrol is simple: freedom and independence. Therefore, the goal of the cooperative communities is to achieve responsible independence and freedom for all.

Within the greater context of a cooperative social model is the facet of our cannabis community. Those from our cannabis community who are experienced in the art of survival in the world of unchecked control freaks understand the necessity of developing, maintaining, and being part of a cooperative community. That is, those who achieved success in the cannabis community did so outside the boundaries established by a tyranny whose intent is our oppression, demonstrating an ability to survive and succeed despite the persecution of an overbearing ruling class.

CANNABIS, ITS COMMUNITY, AND ITS POTENTIAL

This essay will examine the role of cannabis and community; broadly define the relative aspects of community; outline and define some of the main problems that plague us; offer a number of potential solutions; and propose suggestions concerning how the cannabis community, and cannabis specifically, is here to help.

To begin with, I'd like to explain why I choose to be a member of the cannabis community. When asked why I choose to consume the good herb and what benefits I get from it, many answers come to mind. One of the primary reasons, and the one most significant to this piece, is because I enjoy the stereoscopic (and therefore broader) view of reality that I am able to achieve through the experience.

The cannabis experience is an altered state of perception compared to one's baseline state, no doubt. Generally, I find my baseline state to be more linear, hierarchical, or left-brained, whereas my altered view tends to be much more nonlinear, creative, imaginative, and right-brained. The combination and comparison of one's baseline state and altered state create a sort of stereoscopic view, which offers a much greater depth of field than any single mode of perception alone.

Ganja is the safest substance known to humans for obtaining an altered state of perception. Dedicated, disciplined meditation is also capable of safely stimulating an altered state of perception, especially for those averse to ingesting a mind-altering substance. Good herb (combined with practice, of course) is capable of helping to deepen one's meditative abilities, as well.

The choice to freely utilize a heightened awareness flies in the face of a ruling class. Aspects of mental and physical control become more apparent to those with access to a broader sense of awareness, making us less susceptible to such control and therefore also more independent. We are far more likely to question (and potentially learn from) authority. This may be one of the main reasons cannabis is deemed taboo by those "in control" of others.

The good herb is capable of aiding people who are attempting to think for themselves. And people who learn to think for themselves do not need the tyranny of forced order. Those who choose to dominate, however, are dependent upon and require docile, unquestioning masses to control and ultimately exploit. The only thing we need from them is to be left alone. Therefore, the goal for us is to become responsibly independent and able to sustain self-sufficiency.

Another very important factor to consider, especially concerning our cannabis community, is that of economics. Economically speaking, our cannabis community is well ahead of the curve. We produce and market a commodity, a currency that literally grows on trees (or bushes, at least). Despite the oppression and persecution of an overbearing dominator class, our demonized (and renewable) commodity holds a value—sometimes equal to the value of gold! Many are willing to spend upwards of the price of gold for the good herb.

The value of cannabis is partly due to its prohibition but not entirely. In Amsterdam, where cannabis prohibition is lax and herb is legally sold in coffeeshops, many herbs are still as expensive, some more so, than gold (for top-quality, highly desirable or rare product). Please note that a similar phenomenon is witnessed in the wine/spirits industry, with rare and unique specialties fetching hundreds, sometimes thousands, of dollars per bottle.

This economic aspect is important, considering what our cannabis community is capable of contributing (and has contributed) to the larger cooperative community. The fact that our cannabis community has been ultimately banned and ostracized from the general population, leading to society's loss of our economic and intellectual contributions, is an obscene tragedy, indeed. Our ostracism has greatly limited our social participation within the status quo, as well.

Suffice it to say that given a fair opportunity in the open market, our cannabis community could contribute greatly on a number of levels. Instead we are shunned from society's fold, hunted, and imprisoned; our property is forfeited, our lives are turned upside down, and we are threatened and demonized. Instead of being allowed to contribute, we are exiled, persecuted, imprisoned, and sometimes killed.

The beast of oppression flexes its powers, attempting to thwart our community. We remain resilient, but our community suffers losses. The calculated persecution of luminaries, entrepreneurs, and activists such as Rene Boje, Tommy Chong, Marc Emery, Carol Gwilt, Steve Kubby, Eddy Lepp, Todd McCormick, Peter McWilliams (R.I.P.), Angel Raich, Michelle Rainey, Ed Rosenthal, Greg Williams, and countless others continues to this day. Since 1970, over twenty-five million people have been arrested and persecuted for cannabis. This madness must end.

Yet, despite the ongoing assaults, we persist. The fact remains that we are a true community and a culture with much to contribute. Realizing this fact can provide both great strength and considerable hope. Our survival, progress, and success as individuals are directly related to the existence of our cannabis community and culture, which is quite vast worldwide.

Cannabis enterprises, from megabusinesses to cottage industries, hold the potential to provide food, fuel, textiles, biomass, chemicals, medicinals, pharmaceuticals, and herbals. Supplying healthy, clean, and green alternatives to toxic and undesirable synthetics and environmentally damaging tactics is a huge need waiting to be met, and cannabis is consistently answering the challenge. Yet we seem to have a way to go, an enlightenment to ignite, before fully actualizing our success.

DEPENDENCE: A ROADBLOCK ON THE PATH TO SELF-DETERMINATION

A number of problems need to be addressed if we are to progress. These problems range in scope and scale from very broad to very specific. After briefly outlining several of what I perceive to be the primary problems plaguing us, I will attempt to offer brief commentary on some potential solutions, many of which involve cannabis and some form of responsible independence.

One of the broader problems in the developed world is the general population's dependence upon the corporate ruling elite. Much of this dependence is material in nature. Commodities such as food, fuel, shelter, clothing, and even water are generally controlled by large conglomerates driven by an insatiable need to generate vast profits. Given the current systems of supply and demand, it is somewhat difficult, but not impossible, to exist outside the status quo.

A prime example of this problem is obvious in the petrochemical and automotive industries. These conglomerates have grown so large and powerful that an alternative to their control seems impossible to achieve. Although alternatives to fossil fuel do exist (such as solar, wind, hydrogen, compressed air, and biodiesel), the corporate entities that profit from oil use their clout to ensure government subsidies and favoritism for their interests but not for alternatives that threaten their profits. And so we consumers are left with few or no options.

However, alternative options do exist, especially for those willing to forgo a little convenience. And cannabis is definitely one of the most viable of these options. Due to its productiveness and adaptability, cannabis has the potential to be a biomass product filling at least part of the demand for energy.

But handling demands for biomass and energy alone doesn't solve another great problem facing humans and all the occupants of planet Earth: vast environmental change due to exploitation and depletion of resources, along with toxic pollution. Much of this environmental breakdown is directly related to combustion of fossil fuels. This, coupled with deforestation and depletion or pollution of other (oceanic, atmospheric, and/or terrestrial) resources, is wrecking our planet's health.

These environmental problems are thoroughly documented and quite obvious to anyone paying attention. We are learning that our planet's past is littered with evidence of species and organisms that were too successful. They depleted their resource base and were exterminated by their own toxic waste—the shit-in-the-nest syndrome. I hope human beings have developed enough common sense and reason to avoid repeating the mistakes of the past. Unfortunately, our insistent dependence on fossil fuels as an energy source is taking us swiftly down the path of choking on our own toxic waste.

Humanity is also plagued by a dependence on the medical and pharmaceutical industries. Many millions of people follow a cycle of becoming dependent upon some form of medication or surgical procedures. Once started, the cycle of dependency on medication and procedures for ailments, ranging from high blood pressure and high cholesterol to insomnia, obesity, anxiety, and depression, becomes conditioned.

Some misdiagnosed ailments, such as depression (which is often confused with the symptoms of cognitive dissonance), are unnecessarily medicated with questionable and not-yet-fully-understood chemicals. Add to this the overuse of antibiotics, vaccines, and various other inocula and antiviral medications, which cause superdiseases to develop, and the curses of medical dependence become even more apparent. The full impact and outcome of this pharmaco-nightmare remain to be seen. Most ailments are treatable via herbal remedies and simple changes in diet and exercise. But there isn't a large profit in that, so. . .

Overindulgence is another gravely serious problem facing human beings. Be it greed for money, power, or fame or overindulgence in food (perhaps the most common over-indulgence with the broadest consequences), nicotine, drugs (including alcohol), gambling, and even ganja (any substance or habit, really), many suffer from an obsessive-compulsive fixation on consumption and habit. Far too many people escape into habit and miss out on their full, true, novel potential. A form of cognitive dissonance (approach-avoidance conflict issues) may be responsible for a large part of this fixated, obsessive-compulsive dilemma, and it's often misdiagnosed as depression.

We are constantly requested and obliged to perform behaviors that we know are detrimental to us. A case in point is automobiles with internal combustion engines dependent on fossil fuels. Anyone who is at least partly aware and who uses any vehicle realizes, at least subconsciously, that this practice is contributing to the degradation of both personal health and environmental quality. Yet we often choose to drive or ride in such vehicles, stimulating that nagging sense of cognitive dissonance, especially at the gas pump, which may potentially trigger an obsessive-compulsive indulgence. The point here is that overindulgence is a self-feeding cycle of habit in need of attention. Once this is recognized, meditation is beneficial in helping to understand the dilemma and find solutions.

Another problem threatening our future is the practice of monoculture and industrial agriculture. By farming huge tracts of land with only a single species of plant, we invite whatever form of pestilence thrives on that species. When we eliminate the predators and deterrents that would naturally control those pests, we're forced to supplement with, and become dependent upon, chemicals, herbicides, pesticides, and fungicides, all of which are often toxic. Organic farming practices coupled with supporting local producers first is a remedy for this problem.

FORCES OBSTRUCTING TRUE FREEDOM

Two institutions threatening our true freedom are fanatical politics and fundamental religiosity. Both are powerful forms of social and, ultimately, personal control; and both involve manipulation of the media (propaganda, primarily through fear and misinformation), hierarchical power structures, and exploitable masses. The combination of the two institutions is proving to be apocalyptic, especially for the cannabis community. We have suffered the oppression of these institutions for millennia. Countless millions have been persecuted and killed simply for trying to live a simpler life.

From the Pharaohs to the Pharisees to the Romans and the Judeo-Christian and Muslim extremists and crusaders, to First Nations genocides and inquisitions, to witch burnings and our modern-day industrial prison state; from tyrannies and oligarchies to theocracies and monarchies; from fascism and Nazism to monolithic governments and corporations and religious institutions—all forms of social control have exploited and nearly conquered human freedom for their gain. The latter-day fascists see the world and all aspects of life and death as a business opportunity. Their standards are such that they see not a terrorist attack or a natural disaster, but a business opportunity; not an educational or health care system, but a business opportunity; not an environment or a sensitive, delicate functioning ecosystem, but a business opportunity; not a war, but a business opportunity. And so the tragedy unfolds.

Politically, the cannabis community is slowly gaining momentum toward social acceptance and our recognition as a culture. Unfortunately, what we mainly struggle against is a systematic demonizing of our culture via misinformation and the propaganda of fear. It's important to note that the key words in politics are *compromise* and *persistence*. Compromise is the political ideal in that it implies bargaining and a meeting of the minds, whereas persistence has become the primary concern of those who merely seek to win or succeed. Given our cultural suppression,

we have been relatively unable to develop a tenable position from which to bargain, and our persistence has yet to be appreciated.

Our community suffers a discomforting catch-22: We cannot overtly acquire the means to our own self-sufficiency until cannabis is legal, and we cannot fully achieve legalization of herb until we have the self-sufficient means. And it is this very catch that the ruling elite exploits against us. Slowly, we do make progress. Slowly, as in three steps forward thwarted by 2.9 oppressed steps backward. Yet we endure. As Dr. Martin Luther King once observed, "We shall match your capacity to inflict suffering with our capacity to endure suffering." To paraphrase, We shall succeed by our sheer capacity to endure.

Religion is another can of worms altogether. Equally as powerful as politics in its reach and effects, religion is more influential in regard to personal moral issues. That is, while politics has more to do with social issues, religious influence is more personal yet equally powerful in its cumulative effect. Many religious leaders prey upon the faith and gullibility of others for their own gain. And the unfortunate people whose faith enables this gullibility are true casualties in the battlefield for souls.

Perhaps the greatest threat from fundamentalist religious control is that of masculine dominance and the oppression or suppression of femininity. Although this danger has been identified and recognized for millennia and its abolition is one of the primary factors currently used worldwide to gauge successful cultural development, the problem continues into the present. Two of the requirements for our greater community of cooperation to fully actualize and succeed are an acceptance, tolerance, and protection of the feminine being (for both women and men) and the emancipation, education, and empowerment of women worldwide. Currently, the status quo dictates that women are generally conditioned to be feminine and submissive, whereas men are conditioned to be masculine and dominant. While not universal, this conditioning has been common worldwide for some time.

I hold the view that women are naturally more complete human beings than men. I could provide almost endless reams of evidence to support my opinion, ranging from genetic and physical differences to women's greater capacity for emotional empathy and compassion. Or consider that the male Y chromosome is an incomplete X chromosome or that women possess naturally greater endurance than men (along with the ability to give birth). Suffice it to say that experienced and independent women are much better suited to guide than men. It may, in fact, be that masculinity's inadequacies compared to femininity can cause the masculine mind-set to dominate. That is, masculinity's general inadequacy compared to femininity is perhaps what causes certain men, conditioned to be masculine, to subjugate the feminine and seek to conquer and control it by controlling the place of women socially, politically, and economically. No single force is more responsible for this oppression than fundamental religiosity.

Archaeological evidence has been uncovered that indicates the existence of successful, advanced societies existing as much as forty thousand years ago. These societies, which persisted up to about ten thousand years ago, seem to have been socially cooperative, agrarian, self-sufficient, artistic, and organized by women. These cultures may have been influenced by psychedelics, such as psilocybin mushrooms. For more information about these ancient societies, check out some of the works by Terence McKenna or Riane Eisler.

SOME POTENTIAL TACTICS AND SOLUTIONS

In essence, con artists are capable of usurping and exploiting both politics and religion. Most con artists exploit one essential fact: Many people, possibly most, who have been conned refuse to admit it. We deny being conned. This egotistical blunder contributes to so much fraud. Here's a ritual precaution to aid in avoiding this problem: Simply greet yourself in the mirror with friendly respect, the kind you'd enjoy receiving from someone in the larger world. Then, while looking yourself directly in the eye, with a healthy self-confidence, say "I have been conned. I have been lied to and brainwashed, and I am going to continue to find out who I really am and what I really want to be." Do this regularly, daily. This ritual can help you scrutinize all potential attempts to control and exploit you. Once the undue distraction of various forms of mind control are recognized, you'll be freer to employ higher levels of skepticism toward your situation and to deprogram and reprogram yourself accordingly.

The connection between independence and an understanding and application of definitive language holds another very powerful and useful personal tactic. As an example, there are two words that I have virtually eliminated from my vocabulary: *blame* and *fault*. The reason is that both words are far more biased than the more neutral term *responsibility*. It is better to ask "Who is responsible?" than to ask "Who is to blame or at fault?" Solutions are more clearly recognizable when the situation is framed in terms of responsibility than when blame and fault are assigned. It allows greater control, along with the option of claiming a certain level of personal responsibility and poten-

tially a greater involvement in solutions. Once again, let's consider our dependence on fossil fuels: If I choose to blame and fault the oil and auto industries for all the dilemmas their actions (or inaction) cause, it tends to distance me from seeing the personal alternatives available to me. On the other hand, if I choose to take responsibility for my actions, I become more apt to recognize the alternatives available to me—in this case, public transportation, alternative fuel sources (such as biodiesel or hydrogen), and alternative power sources (such as fuel cells, electricity, or compressed air).

Solutions to all of our dilemmas are available but finding them may require a focus that isn't influenced by the distractions of hype and spin, profit, and the bottom line. Now more than ever it is very important to pay attention to what is going on in one's life and out in the larger world. And once the correct direction is recognized, one must pursue it. Lifestyle alone is an extremely significant realm, and the example of a person living in accord with their values can inspire social change. As great passive resistance activists have said, "Let me become the change in the world I wish to see. Let it begin with me."

It is important to remember that in all of the cosmos there is no permanence. Everything is in a constant state of flux and change. Therefore, it is also important to remember that enlightenment, like perfection, is a process, an education, a direction, and not a destination or be-all and end-all. Learning to accept this is the first step toward a necessary realization. Following through with enlightenment then becomes a lifestyle.

Starting with a very broad view of the big picture, I've encountered a simple philosophy on which to build. For me, life has one major rule and the rule has one major clause. I call it the Golden Rule with the Platinum Clause:

1. Life is to be enjoyed.
1a. Not at the expense of another.

It's simple, really, but as serious as can be. The Golden Rule, although seemingly unbalanced toward hedonism, has the Platinum Clause there for balance. Hedonism that isn't achieved at another's expense is a good thing.
I've often pondered the massive amounts of energy put into the cosmos and our place of perception in it and wondered why—the famous "What is the meaning of life?" question. Applying the Golden Rule and Platinum Clause to the equation brought me a great epiphany. It simply makes sense.

It is important to note that life's enjoyment does not merely apply to one's self but to all beings, including the planet as a whole. Suffering is the opposite of enjoyment. It is one's duty to address all suffering found directly on one's path. It is also quite beneficent to promote enjoyment in others. Which brings us back to cannabis.

Another reason I choose to consume cannabis is for its consistent stimulation of a sense of celebration, especially when it's shared. It is important to note here that what one views as enjoyment and celebration is personal and, ideally, unique and individual. Whatever one chooses, or does not choose, for personal enjoyment is fine by me, as long as the Platinum Clause is observed. As the saying goes, Whatever floats your boat.

For me, the good herb—and this is one of the primary tests for truly good herb—usually provides that feeling of "a warm and fuzzy hug from within," as an old friend once put it. With cannabis I have been able to enhance a great deal of enjoyment in life, and not at all at the expense of another, especially if I grow my own. This brings us to what I like to refer to as R.I.S.S-S.

R.I.S.S-S. stands for "Responsible Independent Sustainable Self-Sufficiency." One of the primary mantras of R.I.S.S-S. is "to live simply so that others may simply live" whenever and wherever possible. R.I.S.S-S., like perfection or enlightenment, is best seen as a learning process, a direction, a lifestyle that involves the acceptance and understanding of various types of information and also usually involves some form of trial and error. This is a good foundation for not being stymied by failure. If at first you don't succeed . . . At any rate, R.I.S.S-S. involves a certain level of education and dedication. And a good education is one of the most valuable things a human being may acquire.

Utilization of technology coupled with the guidance of the ancient ways offers us a path to a responsible and sustainable independence. Remember to apply the Golden Rule and Platinum Clause to keep it responsible. A simple example of R.I.S.S-S. applied to a relevant scenario is that of efficiently generating electric power. Much energy is wasted during production and transmission of electricity, in the form of heat lost during the production of electricity and power lost to resistance during transmission. A simple solution is to produce electricity (or other forms of energy) locally, at the community level, and to utilize the heat created locally as well. This solution is not realistically possible as long as the power companies' primary motivation is profit and consumers insist on remaining tied in to the current power grid.

Other, more simple examples of R.I.S.S-S. include organic gardening and composting; recycling and reusing to eliminate waste; and biofuels, hybrid (fuel cell), and hydrogen technologies for the transportation and power industries. By thinking creatively and adopting basic techniques for living simply, we can generate countless other R.I.S.S-S. solutions and paths.

Vegetarianism is another very simple tactic that does much to improve both personal health and the overall health and well-being of the planet. It is a well-known fact that it takes up to nineteen parts of vegetable protein to produce one part of animal protein. For those interested in the purest of the purists' forms of vegetarianism, look into the raw food movement, which advocates the eating of foods that are not heated beyond the point where their enzymes break down. Vegetarianism is truly a beneficent means toward responsible independence.

Perhaps one of the most powerful tactics available to us, especially the audience of this book, is to grow as much good herb as humanly possible. For those of us in the know, producing good herb is the goal. Aside from the insane laws that persecute cannabis growers, there is no downside to producing good herb. Gardening in general is very therapeutic and satisfying, be it for food, fuel, or fiber. Gardening the good herb takes the experience to whole new levels of enjoyment and is a very positive form of R.I.S.S-S. Gardening anything organically is a very powerful tool toward a simple, responsible independence. I would like to take a moment to tell a little story about the current popularity of organic gardening and its more recent origins and reincarnations in the communes of the 1960s and 1970s.

The Contributions of the Communes of the 1960s and 1970s

Beyond the social circuit of passing a joint, the roots of our community sprouted in the farming and free lifestyle communes of the 1960s and 1970s. These communes were a natural phenomenon greatly inspired by masses of people choosing to question the validity of their prior conditioning. Our community began to self-actualize a responsible self-sufficiency in these early communes.

The 1960s was a decade when a door in the wall of human suppression was unlocked and opened. The backlog of experience that had piled up behind that door for so many centuries came spilling out dramatically. Those years were often hectic and chaotic, and the experiences produced by an era of raw freedom were many and varied. Raw freedom existed prior to the 1960s, of course, but opportunities to experience it were few and far between. By the 1960s, several circumstances forced a close of this raw freedom into the mainstream. This freedom grew and progressed into and through the 1970s and beyond. One facet of this freedom was the sexual revolution.

This sexual revolution contributed to the broadening of consciousness in much the same way cannabis did—by providing a view and experience of reality different from the accepted and allowed norm. Women, the primary beneficiaries of the sexual revolution, experienced a freedom unequaled for thousands of years, thanks in part to gaining control of reproductive rights. The pill, along with other means of contraception and birth control, fueled a grand broadening of mores and boundaries previously kept tightly constrained by pious and bigoted religious and political leaders.

Men were also beneficiaries of the sexual revolution, although more in terms of a hedonistic and self-serving sense of pleasure. Free love held more consequences for women than for men, as it is primarily women who need to deal with the realities of childbearing. Some women chose the responsibility of child-bearing and, as a result, it was mainly women who organized, began, and contributed most to the first free lifestyle communes of the 1960s and 1970s. Women saw the need for a responsible, self-sustaining environment in which to raise the children born of the free love movement.

These early communes were foundations of knowledge and enlightenment. They focused on living a responsible, independent, self-sufficient, and sustainable lifestyle. Some of the more famous ones were the Farm in Tennessee (Stephen and Ina May Gaskin), the "Om Farm" in California (Reggae on the River), the Alpha Farm in Oregon, the Hog Farm (Wavy Gravy, the Pignic, Earthdance), and Ruigaard in Holland, to name a few. But many smaller and equally successful ventures developed up and down the West Coast of North America, in the U.S. hinterlands, and in rural Europe. Some urban enclaves also existed, such as the Provos in Amsterdam or the artist/free speech communities in Greenwich Village, Berkeley, and San Francisco. Initially, the going was very rough for the rugged individuals who cleared the way so that others might follow. Trial and error ruled the process, and success was finally achieved by tapping into the ancient knowledge of indigenous cultures not destroyed by the usurpers' conquest. Much of that knowledge involved methods of organic gardening. Unconditional love also contributed greatly, as many gave so much with little or no expectation of compensation other than the success of the freedom movement.

Among those who seek, it's common knowledge that the production and trade of cannabis provided the economic under-pinnings necessary for the development and survival of the early communes. Cannabis was one of the keys used to unlock the chains that bound us to the status quo of the time.

The gardens of these early communes are where many of the organic farming methods used today were resurrected, learned, practiced, refined, and perfected. Sustainable agricultural techniques borrowed from antiquity proved very successful, especially concerning the quality of the produce.

The first successful communes showed us that we might achieve independence from controlling social structures while also increasing our overall enjoyment of life. Much of this independence is directly related to organic methods of agriculture: composting, companion planting, breeding for success, and avoidance of toxic chemicals and mono-cultures, as well as an openness toward bioregionalism.

Often referred to as the "counterculture," upon closer examination one is able to witness how we are, in fact, the true primary source of current Western culture. Due to our many successes in developing a self-sustaining and responsible society, our culture developed and progressed, while the systems of the status quo, dependent upon the exploitation of the masses, falters. Therefore, those of us who choose the responsible, self-sustaining ways are the true "culture" (indicating healthy independent growth), whereas those who choose the exploitative ways of domination, empire, and control are like a cancer feeding upon the benefits of our development.

The early communes broke free of the status quo, explored the alternatives, and found the successes necessary to survive independently. But independence comes with a price: One must be willing to leave the often cozy confines of one's conditioning and learn a new way of living. The initial period of learning the alternative is the hard part. Once committed to and practiced, the alternatives often prove much simpler to live than one's original conditioning within the status quo. Organic agriculture, an important alternative for our increasingly toxic planet, was one outgrowth of the communes; another important concept that sprouted from the cultural awareness they inspired is bioregionalism.

Bioregionalism

Bioregionalism defines a means by which people seeking to live a more responsible self-sufficiency may be best able to do so. According to *The Canadian Oxford Compact Dictionary*, a bioregion is "an area or region that constitutes a natural ecological community." Acting locally is bioregionalism's key concept, primarily concerning what we consume or produce. Generally speaking, a bioregion that exists within a continental landmass is defined by the different watersheds and the environments and species that naturally exist within them. Therefore, it is the high ground and mountain ridges that naturally divide region from region.

An example from the Pacific Northwest of North America would be the Columbia River and all of its drainage systems, including the Willamette and Snake Rivers—one of the more massive regions. Those living in the Columbia drainage who choose to practice bio-regionalism would produce and consume the local native species, such as salmon, hazelnuts, camas bulbs, timber, local berries and fruits, indigenous mushrooms, and so on.

By producing and collecting native species, one can take advantage of the same circumstances that the native species utilize. Toxic chemicals are not necessary, and certain levels of monoculture are acceptable, especially if some form of companion planting is utilized. (Companion planting is the art of growing various species of plants that are beneficial to each other together.)

Cannabis, though historically indigenous to Indo-Asian regions, is well suited to bio-regional demands as there are so many different phenotypes capable of uniquely acclimating to almost any region on the planet. Good for industrial, medicinal, and agricultural purposes, cannabis is waiting patiently to responsibly and cleanly serve our needs. We in the cannabis community are again at the forefront of revolution in our ability to provide commodities that are far more environmentally sound. We accomplished this feat almost entirely outside the boundaries established by the status quo and ruling elite. We have figured out a way.

So many cannabis and hemp products are available now—too many to name them all, with more continually available. Supporting our community is one of the simplest ways to assure our success. Products such as Blackspot shoes, brought to us by Adbusters, are the wave of the conscious, sustainable future; eco-friendly, they're made of recycled or natural materials (rubber tires and hemp) by union, not sweatshop, workers in places such as Portugal. But production is only half of the equation for successful bioregionalism. The other half is consumption. Perhaps one of the primary tenets of bioregionalism is to support one's local community first and foremost. This practice is simple common sense and spreads beyond mere concepts of region.

SOME TACTICAL ADVICE FOR LATTER-DAY ASPIRING ACTIVISTS, LUMINARIES, VISIONARIES, HEADS, AND WHAT-HAVE-YOUS

I appreciate and feel fortunate to have had some great advice from those who forged our path. From Ken Kesey to Carlos Castaneda, luminaries from the recent past have left us a great archive and resource of knowledge. Timothy Leary was one such cage rattler. Tim Leary had an effective chutzpah; however, in my opinion, he got the order of his "tune in, turn on, drop out" mantra backward. Nowadays, I'd recommend that one first drop out, even if only for an afternoon or a weekend at a time. Then, while dropped out, tune in to what one finds (ideally something alternative to what one dropped out of). Finally, if one is lucky after tuning in, turn on to what one finds there. This has worked very well for me.

Ken Kesey, another doorman for consciousness, did a great job in the skin he was in. I appreciate Ken's logic in his personal assertion to "always stay in your own movie." Ah, Ken, he understood the Platinum Clause long before I did. To me, staying in one's own movie means simply staying on one's own personal path and dealing with that which is upon that path—simple common sense.

Another piece of sage advice of great value is the adage "always keep (that is, never lose) your cool." There are two sayings that go together well: "If they get to you, they got to you." and "Don't let them get to you." Good mantras both, very handy at times, and a valuable reminder in times of need. It is okay to fear; fear is natural. The trick is to stay clear, to remain in control of your focus. Our oppressors use our fear and anger against us, but this is not possible when people are in control of their focus. Remember also that rights are like muscles: virtually useless unless exercised. So become inspired to go out into the world and be active, and remember to always keep your cool. Don't let them get to you.

GOVERNMENT

Like it or not, we will need to do something about government if we are to succeed as a species. Ideally, the role of good government would be to provide for and protect its people and environment. Good government would also ideally be completely transparent and accessible by all of its citizens. Unfortunately, most of our ruling bodies are a far cry from this ideal. Current governments seem only to be concerned with establishing and maintaining their power base. The U.S. Constitution once boasted being "of the people, by the people, and for the people," but sadly, the American government has become "of the special interests, by the corporations, and for the wealthy." Currently, it feels as though the only recourse for commoners, or working class people, is to either support or become one of those categories—special interests, corporations, or the wealthy.

A specific problem with current ruling bodies is the obscene amount of power they wield. Another problem involves the levels of fear that are apt to dictate government protocols. The combination of these two problems is indeed nearly overwhelming. Bureaucratic leaders use fear as a means of ensuring their power base. Threats of war, terrorism, natural disaster, disease, moral decay, and so on, are used as propaganda to instill fear in the masses, as an excuse to eliminate our rights, freedoms, and liberty, and as justification for the need for the government's very existence. But perhaps those who allow fear to occlude their reason shouldn't be making decisions on behalf of the rest of us. As for the power issue, perhaps we could at least examine the circumstances and agree to never again allow the levels of power that inspired the frenzy of corruption and greed that have existed and do exist today.

I see the need for an active form of government on two levels: community and global. All other forms of government—city, county/parish/district, state/provincial/canton, and national—perhaps would function best as conduits of communication between local and global levels. The community would act and respond locally, while the global institutions would protect communities, primarily from conquest but also in the event of a natural disaster or any crisis.

Personally, I find the concept of "leaders" very counterproductive—I have little time for people who need to follow. Ideally, if people had full access to relevant information, they would be less dependent upon institutions and much more independent. The Internet is a good resource, despite the high signal-to-noise ratio one needs to endure in order to find relevant, valid, and reliable information. But the information is out there, in many different forms, for those who actively seek. The key, again, is responsible independence.

CANNABIS IS HERE TO HELP

In review, we all choose our own path and the communities to which we belong. Our cooperative community hopes to succeed by offering a responsible, independent, and sustainable self-sufficiency for all who choose this path. Our cannabis community hopes to succeed by contributing to the overall success of cooperative communities, both economically and, given a fair opportunity in the open market, as a clean, renewable resource worthy of responsible production. Cannabis is here to help.

Cannabis is the safest substance known to humans for altering consciousness. An altered state of consciousness is capable of offering deeper creative insight and broader perception, if approached responsibly. This heightened awareness is at times capable of revealing viable alternatives and creative solutions that would perhaps otherwise remain unseen. When focused toward responsible independence, this heightened awareness is capable of rendering dominating controllers useless and moot.

Many of the problems plaguing us—from environmental degradation to codependency with conglomerates, from overindulgence all the way to empire, dynasty, and manifest destiny—are still solvable. There is still time. Even the more deeply rooted problems such as fanatical politics, fundamental religiosity, and the dominance and oppression of the feminine worldwide have solutions. Alternatives exist for those who endure the inconvenience of finding and living them.

There are tactics and solutions, many alternative but a few mainstream, available to those who seek. Understanding the power and definitive meaning of language is key, as is the healthy self-confidence necessary to deprogram and reprogram one's self to be who one truly is and wants to be. Remember that this is an ongoing process that will ideally become a lifestyle.

Remember to apply the Golden Rule and the Platinum Clause (1. Life is to be enjoyed and 1.a. Not at the expense of another) to your lifestyle to ensure that a proper dose of R.I.S.S-S. (Responsible Independent Sustainable Self-Sufficiency) is maintained for the good of all. Research and review all of the pertinent information from the past available to you (there is a great deal of it). Search for and find information from the early communes, especially concerning organic farming and bioregionalism. And use what you learn to grow as much really good herb as you possibly can. When you do, please give me a shout and let me help judge! Remember, cannabis is here to help.

INTRODUCTION

People often ask me why I wrote the Cannabibles. It certainly wasn't to get rich; if that had been my aim, I would have chosen to be a grower! The reasons I created the books are numerous, but the most important reason by far is to help raise the quality of cannabis *globally*. My goal is to do this by educating growers and smokers alike by showing them what is ultimately possible, and by sharing the things I've learned on my blessed journey into the cannabis universe. In this volume of the series, I have really focused on this goal. I am very proud of this Cannabible. I hope you enjoy reading it as much as I enjoyed making it.

My work seems to be having a positive effect, as I get emails all the time from people telling me things like "Thanks to what I learned in the Cannabibles, I no longer get headaches [paranoid, stupified, lethargic, *whatever* when I smoke." Quite a few growers have told me that they've switched to organics based on what they read in the Cannabibles, and that their herb is much more enjoyable now. I *really* love those emails! In fact, I consider them my pay. (Free nugs are always nice too!)

When I first started working on the Cannabibles, I was just a guy with a camera trying to convince growers—some of the most paranoid folks on the planet—to show me their most private spot in the world: their ganja garden. At times, this proved rather difficult. As the years progressed, I became more known and trusted in the cannabis community, and more gardens started opening up to me. Give thanks! After the first Cannabible came out, which took about six years to complete, everything changed. People from all around the world began contacting me with invitations to photograph their gardens, some of which were truly spectacular.

I became much more familiar with the strains that people were growing by paying extremely close attention to details as well as by working with them myself, and in the process I became aware of the inherent difficulties in trying to catalog the world's finest cannabis strains. In short, I found that with any given bud, I was judging the grower more than the strain itself. And the unfortunate reality is that the horticultural skills of most growers leave a lot to be desired, to put it politely. I have come across certain strains a half dozen times or more and not been particularly impressed, and then I get a batch expertly grown by a truly masterful organic cultivator, and *holy cow*, it's brilliant and barely resembles the stuff from the less-skilled growers.

To make matters even more confusing, I've found that even if the grower does a great job, I am really only reviewing one particular phenotype of the given strain. (The phenotype is the observable physical or biochemical characteristics of an organism, as determined by both genetic makeup and environmental influences.) This single well-grown phenotype doesn't necessarily reflect what a person would end up with if they grew out a pack of seeds. Even the nutrients used greatly affect the flavor and character of the herb, adding to the difficulty of fairly reviewing any given strain. And outdoor gardens present yet another set of variables, as local and seasonal variations, such as rain, can greatly affect the finished product.

I soon figured out that the only way I could evaluate all the different strains in a fair way was to grow them all myself. Impossible, unless one of two things were to happen:

1. I'd have to put far fewer strains in each volume.

2. I'd have to work on each book for fifteen years and never travel, which in itself would severely limit the project. Plus, if I grew all the strains myself, the books would look fairly repetitive, and the reader would still be seeing only what those particular phenotypes looked like when grown in the way I chose, in the environment that I chose. This would not necessarily reflect what another person would end up with if they grew a pack of seeds from the same strain.

So you can see the difficulty. It's all so subjective, there are so many variables, and the plant in question is a highly adaptable species capable of endless permutations. I've found that a skilled grower can actually grow fine herb from average genetics, but a bad grower could have the best genetics on the planet and still grow mediocre herb. At the same time, the best grower in the world can't grow truly great herb from low-quality genetics, but an inexperienced grower can get lucky and pull off some great herb with top-rate genetics. I've even found that if you take ten clones from the same mother plant and give them to ten different growers, you'll end up with ten surprisingly different-looking and different-tasting herbs (there are plenty of examples of this in the Cannabibles). I gave a Dutch, commercially grown sample of Top 44 a terrible review in *Cannabible 1*, but years later I came across a piece of it grown organically by an expert, and it was actually pretty good! I've found that with most of the strains currently grown, an expert cultivator could grow delicious and stony herb. The point I'm making is that due to all the things I've mentioned, plus the fact that the plant is illegal in most of the world, there is a massive gray area that I must work within to make these books. There is no perfect solution that's feasible.

But what I can do these days is utilize the amazing online cannabis community that didn't exist when I started making these books. Overgrow.com* has been a huge help in the Cannabible-making process in recent years, as it allows me to see what countless other people, some of them very advanced growers and connoisseurs, have to say about the various strains and seed banks. I'm also fortunate to work with a core group of very advanced growers in documenting these strains—folks who have proven to me that they are true master cultivators and can bring out the best in each strain. They are all small-scale medical growers, so quantity and variety often take the backseat to quality, but that's a huge plus in my book (and in my books). I

am very happy with the strains represented in *The Cannabible 3*. They are truly some of the best out there, and most were grown by true master cultivators. When possible and appropriate, I've shown multiple versions or phenotypes of a strain to help you understand the effects of environment, growing techniques, and phenotype selection.

Though you may think I have the best job in the world, in truth, you're right! But it's often difficult. For example, when a seed company I like puts out a strain that I don't like, I have to be honest. If I wasn't, I'd be no better than the corrupt government systems that I so often criticize. (For example, corporations giving money to politicians—their "friends"—who then pass laws that benefit these companies; as a result, our planet is trashed and our society severely harmed.) I can't stoop to that level. If a certain company gives me some free nugs, or perhaps even sells lots of my books, I still have to be honest when I review their strain, even if it sucks. I've lost friends over things like this before, but I simply must tell the truth. And speaking of telling it like it is, read on . . .

ALTERNATIVE *EVERYTHING*

Recently I have come to an incredibly disturbing conclusion. There is no nice way to say it, so I'll just put it out there: Across the board, almost all of the underpinnings of our "civilization" are poisonous and destructive, not only to us but to our environment and our only home, the planet earth, as well. This might seem preposterous to many of you, and if someone had said this to me fifteen years ago, I would have thought it a bit extreme myself. But I see it so painfully clearly now. It seems that everything from the "food" we eat, the water we drink, and the fibers we wear to the fuel we use, the materials our houses and workplaces are built from, and the "medicines" our doctors and dentists use and prescribe—*everything*—is poisonous.

For one example, let's take a look in the average supermarket. If you go into a typical grocery store in most of the world, the vast majority of products are simply not worth consuming. Instead of healthful food, what you find is row after row of dead, processed, devitalized, genetically modified, irradiated, chemically grown garbage. Even if you go to the produce section, the truth about most of what's there is disturbing. For one thing, most the fruits and vegetables are commercially grown, which means that literally tons of harmful carcinogenic chemicals (pesticides, herbi-

*Update on overgrow.com and cannabisworld.com: These websites, mentioned in *Cannabible 3* several times, are down now and the situation needs to be addressed—our community is suffering! The Canadian authorities took down the websites because Heaven's Stairway seed company, which was busted in early 2006 owns them. The latest word is that the Canadian authorities never took the servers, that all the info is still there, and that the sites will likely be put back up sometime relatively soon, most likely in a different country. A trial is pending.

cides, and fertilizers) were used to raise them from the dead soil in which they were grown.

Also, please realize that most of that commercial fruit was grown somewhere on the other side of the planet, picked early, shipped across oceans (using fossil fuels), only to somehow arrive looking passable but lacking any vibrancy nonetheless. Did you know that the average food item travels 2,500 miles before it reaches your plate? The powers that be have even taken the one thing that you'd think was unquestionably healthy—lettuce—and turned it into useless roughage: iceburg lettuce! Literally void of nutrients, it is, sadly, the most commonly eaten green in America! Those flawless oranges with deeply colored skins? That is *not* what oranges look like in the real world! The tomatoes? Genetically engineered! The scary thing is, we have no idea whatsoever what effect GM foods have on human health, but the initial reports are not reassuring. In the only serious scientific study of the effects of eating GM foods, results showed that the engineered gene transferred from a soy burger and a soy milkshake to bacteria in the human gut after a single meal. And since the introduction of U.S.-grown soy to the UK, soy allergies have skyrocketed there by about 50 percent!

Even something as seemingly pure and innocuous as water, sacred giver of life, is problematic. Those endless bottles on grocery store shelves contain dead, lifeless water bottled somewhere thousands of miles away only to arrive at the store sterile and lifeless. It can keep you alive, but it won't properly hydrate you. (Read about living water to learn more.) They turned sugar, which in its whole form is quite healthful, into white sugar, probably the most harmful drug on the planet. Or consider wheat: Many people have difficulty digesting wheat even in its whole form. But once it's made into the ubiquitous white flour it becomes poisonous gunk that blocks up the colon and digestive system. And since the process of "refining" wheat into white flour removes almost all of it's nutrients, it then becomes necessary to "enrich" it—using synthetic and harmful chemicals!

Now that our soils and the foods grown on them have become so depleted, and because much of what people eat is refined, processed food, it's recommended that you to take vitamin and mineral supplements, most of which are chemically derived and contain petroleum byproducts that are incredibly harmful to your organs and immune system, to say the least. This is why you pee really yellow when you take them—because the elements in them are completely unusable by the human body and actually stress and tax your organs and immune system as they try to pass them through. (Look for vitamins that say "bioavailable"

on the label. This means that your body can actually use them.) In other words, not only are these "vitamins" not good for you, they are quite bad for you! It's scary to think that food, something we consume and incorporate into our bodies on a daily basis, has become so unhealthful, both for us and for our planet. So what can you do about all of these problems with food? First, remember that your dollar is your vote—perhaps the strongest one you have (as the 2004 elections seemed to indicate). Whenever possible, eat organic foods. Consider growing an organic garden yourself, or participate in an organic community supported agriculture (CSA) enterprise. And if you really want to make a difference, here's the big one: Eat lower on the food chain. Raising animals for human consumption leads to staggering amounts of water pollution, greenhouse gases (methane), deforestation, and erosion. It's estimated that 70 percent of the crops grown in the United States are fed to animals, not humans. If we were to eat the grains fed to stock animals instead of eating the animals, vast tracts of land could be restored to a natural state.

The problems with our current system certainly aren't confined to our food supply. The building materials our homes and places of work are made from are equally tainted. Treating wood with the poison arsenic to preserve it is a common practice throughout the Western world. Asbestos is another killer that surrounds us, and of all things most of the municipal water pipes in the United States are made of asbestos cement. And not so ironically, the carpets in your house and the interior of your car are almost guaranteed to be coated with chemicals from none other than DuPont, one of the primary pushers for the illegalization of marijuana. (For more information on the "drug wars," read *The Emperor Wears No Clothes* by Jack Herer.)

Our water supplies have been contaminated by agricultural chemicals, industrial pollutants, and all manner of insults. Then, to add injury to insult, it's treated with more chemicals to make it "safe" for drinking, most notably chlorine, which then reacts with organic chemicals in the water to produce highly toxic trihalomethanes. So if you can't trust the water, what can you trust? Certainly not the pharmaceuticals that Western society lives (and dies) by—*all poison*. Do they really cure anything? Not that I have observed. They're nothing more than a chemical Band-Aid, and most of the conditions they're meant to cure are just the ills of our dysfunctional civilization. Most drugs don't address the causes of disease at all, but instead mask the symptoms, making it harder for us to understand what's really going on and what the ultimate causes of disease are. And in reality, many drugs only weaken the immune system even further, thus actually decreasing the body's innate ability to heal. Commercial shampoos, conditioners, soaps, sunblocks, and all the other products we slather on our permeable skin (our body's largest organ) are full of poisonous chemicals. It seems as though these chemical corporations have infiltrated just about every aspect of our lives.

Meanwhile, since the introduction of all these chemicals into every facet of our lives ("better living through modern chemistry—not!"), all kinds of cancers have skyrocketed. Most people don't even think twice about all the chemicals in their lives, let alone understand the correlation between these chemicals and the modern epidemic of cancers and other diseases. This way of life has become so normalized that it really seems, well, normal. Let me tell you people, this is not normal, much less good, and it is certainly not "God's plan"!

As a rule of thumb, if you can't identify or even pronounce the ingredients in a product you're considering buying or using, pass it by. Instead, go to the health food store! The great news is that there are fantastic natural alternatives to *all* of these chemical products. You might spend a little more for organic and natural products, but I assure you you'll save all of it and more on hospital bills later. And while organic foods cost more up front, they are nutritionally far superior to chemically grown foods, as well as much safer for the environment, so when you look at the ultimate bottom line—survivability—they definitely cost less. Plus, if more people supported organic farming, it would become even more affordable.

I am pleased to tell you that I am not just preaching out of my butt; I am a living example of how we can live in a healthier way. My house gets its electricity from the sun. In the thirteen years the system has been up, it's already more than paid for itself. (No electricity bills!) My water comes from the sky in the form of rain and is heated by a solar heater that sits on my roof. My Jeep Liberty CRD runs on 100 percent biodiesel fuel, which is recycled vegetable oil collected locally. It costs 50 cents less per gallon than gasoline and doesn't entail the karma attached to supporting a system that sends brainwashed youth off to die (and kill) for cheap oil. I wear all-natural fibers, mostly hemp (of course). I eat about 99 percent organic foods. And I feel and look a hell of a lot better now. I swear that I say this not to brag or gloat, but to hopefully inspire.

People are scared to change for a lot of reasons, but a big one is because they think going "green" will cost more. While it might in the short term, I assure you that in the long term it does not. In the end, when all the facts are in, it costs less. These changes haven't been difficult or expensive for me to make. In fact, knowing what I know now, it would be insane for me to have not made these changes!

It's simply a matter of balance. There's no way to be 100 percent pure unless you're Woody Harrelson, and even Woody isn't entirely pure. So we have to acknowledge that we're all going to absorb some amount of poisons, but let's process, metabolize, and eliminate them. As citizens of the modern world, we're all probably going to accrue at least a bit of environmental karma, too, but let's do everything we can to minimize our negative impact on the world. Again, at this point in time, this planet is our only home. Let's do what we can to keep it healthy.

It isn't easy for me to make these accusations against my own "culture." In fact, you might be wondering why this rant is even included in this Cannabible. Well I'll tell you: Smoking cannabis is what opened my eyes, as well as many others' eyes, to seeing all this stuff so clearly, and it changed my life. *And the powers that be know it! They know cannabis is a revolutionary substance, and that's the main reason it's illegal!*

I've always felt that cannabis is a gift from the Goddess, a tool that's been given to us to help us evolve, expand our consciousness, and become more spiritual beings. It's been given to us to help us wake up. And it *is* time to wake up, friends! I'm sure many of you can see that we're living in dark times right now. There is a massive effort under way to keep us in spiritual ignorance, to keep our vibration down. Vibration lowering is the thread that runs through all of it. Cannabis raises the vibration, which is the main reason it is illegal, along with other psychedelics that also expand consciousness and raise the vibration. "They" don't like drugs that raise the vibration. "They" like drugs that lower the vibration, such as alcohol, cigarettes, and pharmaceuticals.

If you're ready to raise your vibration, not just by using cannabis but also by bucking the system, here's a list of some of the things that lower our vibrations and should be avoided as much as possible:

All commercial foods
Most cooked foods
Preservatives
Artificial flavorings
Artificial colorings
All white "food" products (sugar, flour, salt, and so on)
The electromagnetic soup we all live in
Genetically modified organisms (GMOs)
Building supplies (especially wood treated with arsenic!)
Cleaning products

Cell phones and their towers
Mercury fillings
Vaccinations and immunizations
Aspartame and other artificial sweeteners
Every show on television (except for a select few
    educational shows)
Television and computer screens
The fuels that power and pollute our lives
Video games
Microwave ovens
School systems
Meat
Alcohol
Cigarettes
Pharmaceutical drugs
Politics
Fried foods
Commercials on TV
Gambling
Chlorine
Fluoride
Most popular music
Pesticides
Herbicides
Chemical fertilizers
All hard drugs
Heavy metals
Polluted, dead water
Polluted air
Cities
Traffic
Synthetic fibers
Most vitamins and supplements
Most body care products
Irradiated foods
CFCs

People, this is a calling out to *take back your vibration!* Here are some things that raise the vibration:

Love
Organic ganja
Organic raw foods
Sprouted foods
Yoga
Meditation
Tai chi
Laughter
Kindness
Lovemaking
Positive thoughts
Exercise
Connection with nature
Massage
Clean, living water
Clean air
Certain kinds of music
Healing with natural remedies
Jerry
Chanting
Psychedelics

We all have the freedom to choose what goes into our bodies. Exercising that freedom will bring you profound well-being, and it will also honor all of those who have have worked, suffered, and even died over the years to protect and preserve that freedom. When you choose what to put into your body and how to live your life, remember that no one can take away that freedom unless you let them. Don't just fall in step with the corporate programming. I highly recommend that you check out the new book by my friend Woody Harrelson, *How to Go Further*. It explains all this and more in greater detail. And lastly, if I had to recommend just one lifestyle change that could make a huge difference in your health and the health of the planet—shop only at health food stores or stores that specialize in natural products.

All of that said, let's get started on the task at hand. Turn the page, hold on to your hat, and get ready to enjoy some of the finest organic, revolutionary, and vibration-raising herb on the planet.

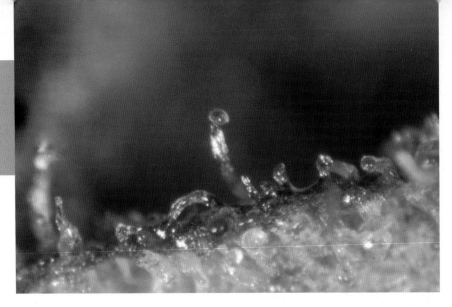

A10

A10 is a compact indica clone that is very common in the California buyers club scene. I believe Ed Rosenthal had something to do with it. This strain, while very beautiful during flowering, was truly unimpressive when smoked. Although the plant has a pleasant though underwhelming fruity, pungent quality when alive, smoking the finished product was a bland and unmemorable experience. The strain is very susceptible to powdery mildew, and every sample I found of **A10** had some mildew, which definitely lowers the quality. The high from this herb is a cloudy light-narcotic feeling, not what I like to smoke. Not recommended. This sample was grown outdoors organically in Mendocino, California.

rootball

Here we have a gorgeous mystery **African** sativa strain crossed with the old standby, **Northern Lights**. This hybrid responded well to the intense Northern California sun, producing giant, fragrantly spicy colas. The exotic smell of the fresh flowers transitioned perfectly all the way to one-year cured herb. The smoke is rich and spicy, robust and earthy. Luckily, she gets her flavor from the **African** side of the equation, as **Northern Lights** is generally not a very flavorful strain. Grown outdoors organically in Mendocino, California.

African x Northern Lights

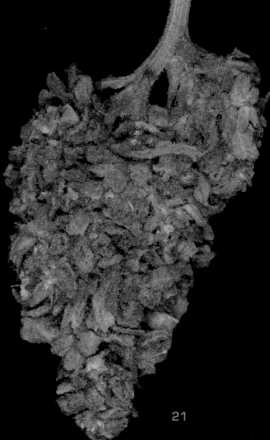

THE GOVERNMENT CANNABIS FARM IN MISSISSIPPI—G-13?

By now many of you have heard that the U.S. government has a marijuana farm and research facility at the University in Oxford, Mississippi. This is the only place in the United States where marijuana is grown completely legally, including federally. This is where they grow the herb that is given to the seven legal recipients of federally grown marijuana under the Compassionate Investigational New Drug (IND) program (see page 54). The legendarily potent G-13 strain was supposed to have been liberated from this farm some time in the late 1970s to early 1980s. No cannabis strain on the planet has more herban legend and rumor associated with it than G-13. Problem is, no one seems to agree on anything with regard to this plant.

Old-timers who claim to have been there swear it's a sativa from Mexico crossed with an Afghani. Others swear it's pure indica. Some are convinced that it was a clone that was taken, while others say no one had cloned marijuana when G-13 hit the scene, so it must have been seeds. Some say it was bred for extremely high potency and a no-ceiling/no-tolerance characteristic, while others say it was the first genetically modified cannabis strain. It has also been said that the project was an effort to enhance the economy of the state of Mississippi through the pharmaceutical industry, by extracting the THC so that drug companies could synthesize its molecular structure. More rumors surround this strain than any other I know.

Many people, myself included, have smoked devastatingly potent buds that were sold as G-13. This I can tell you for sure: The cannabis the government grows is crap. I've seen it a few times, and it smells and tastes like hemp and has about the same THC content. It's mostly leaves and stems. People who toured the government farm (back when a tour was still offered) report that the plants they saw growing were definitely sativa dominant. So if the government did create the compact and superpotent strain that many know as G-13, they did it in a secret indoor facility and have never made public any information on the project. I am skeptical, to be honest. There are several different clones called G-13 going around, and a plethora of hybrids as well. If a clone had been stolen, one would think there would still be just the one version. But alas, there are several. The one probably seen the most these days is known as Airborne G-13, pictured here growing in Northern California. I have no idea what *Airborne* is supposed to mean.

A gentleman has recently come forward who claims to know the real truth about G-13. He says that he met a girl in the 1980s who had the real-deal G-13, and that she said her boyfriend worked at a government lab that was testing/breeding the herb. After hearing the whole story, it did seem believable. The lineage is reported to be Acapulco Gold crossed with Afghani, which also is believable. The story goes that this plant was chosen because it was a *sport*, which means that it showed mutations

airborne g13 clone
from pacific seed co.

g13

(in this case beneficial) that could be passed down to the next generation. It was a scraggly plant with pathetic yields, but it had one very desirable trait —proliferous resin production!

From this freak, G-13 was supposedly bred, and the legends and rumors continue to this day. G-13: superpotent government bud or marketing ploy used to up the value of some bland Afghani? We may never know, but the bottom line is this: The stuff doesn't taste that great, and the high just puts most people to sleep—not what I'm looking for! G-13 produces unusually round nugs and has an odd fruity and musty smell. The flavor is lacking, which is a major detractor in my book. This sample was grown outdoors in Northern California and is of the Airborne G-13 clone.

bubba kush x airborne g13

Is this where g13 was bred?

23

indoor organic soil

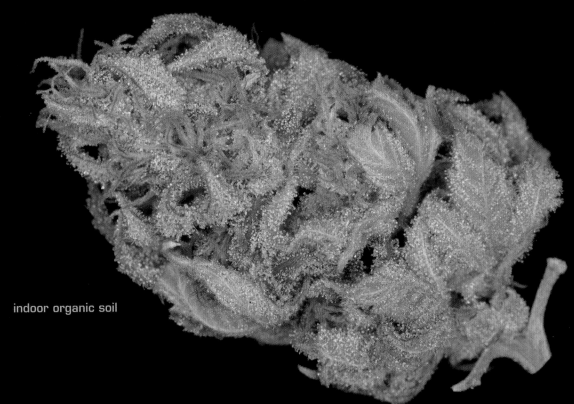

indoor organic soil

24

Albert Walker

Albert Walker is an extremely rare elite clone originating in the Pacific Northwest. No one seems to know anything of its lineage, though the strain is for real and is absolutely amazing. It's a medium-sized plant with an Afghani-dominant growth pattern, a bit finicky to dial in and a major nutrient hound, but highly worth the effort. When growing, Albert Walker reeks of lemony roadkill skunk, with many other aromas that words do not exist for. Yield is actually pretty good on this one, and harvest can be expected indoors in about sixty-five days. The flavor of the Walker is spectacular and unique, albeit nearly impossible to describe. It's tangy yet semi-rotten, almost menthol-like and not quite astringent but something close. It's slightly reminiscent of OG Kush but with a whole other world of flavors. A deep inhalation of a freshly ground-up nug leaves you with a giant smile and a tingly nose. The high from Albert Walker is exceptional and one of my very favorites. It's extremely euphoric and happy—you cannot be in a bad mood when high on Albert Walker. Although it's very strong, it's not debilitating—unless, of course, you can't stop giggling. For an hour or so after smoking some, I get little tingly rushes from head to toe. I look forward to seeing this highly coveted strain made more available.

Asian Fantasy

The good news is that **Asian Fantasy**, arguably the tastiest herb I've ever smoked, is actually still alive (see *Cannabible 1*, page 32, for a full strain description). The bad news is that the only person who has it is a "strain hoarder," and he won't give it up. It's likely that he'll lose it soon, as his attempts at growing it indoors have been less than successful. I've been telling him for years, to no avail, that some strains just need to be grown outdoors. This is the only phenotype of **Asian Fantasy** still alive as far as I know. This batch was about a third as flavorful as the outdoor Asian Fantasy featured in *Cannabible 1*, but it was unmistakable Asian Fantasy. You never forget that flavor. These flowers were grown indoors organically in soil in Northern California. Please do not bogart cannabis strains. Spread the love!

indoor organic soil

indoor organic soil
different grower

<< Banana

This is another relatively new clone making its way around the West Coast, particularly among indoor growers in the Humboldt area. The strain does very well indoors, quickly producing fat and heavy colas of sappy, dank bud. The flavor definitely reminds me of sappy dried bananas, with a dank bottom end reminiscent of Big Bud. Pictured are samples grown hydroponically and in organic soil. The organic one, predictably, was far superior in every way.

hydro

Belladonna

If you're a Skunk fan, you may like **Belladonna**. She seems a typical Dutch Skunk variety (translation: boring). To be honest, this strain from Paradise Seeds in Amsterdam left me craving something with more flavor. The flavor is lightly skunky with soft herbal tones. The high? Decent, but nothing to write home about. I would bet anything that if this strain were cultivated masterfully, I would have liked it much more. I will say this: Paradise is one of the most respected seed companies around, for good reason.

This old-school Northern California indica is a very trippy strain indeed. The smell is earthy and vitaminy, reminiscent of good Thai bud. The flavor, however, lies somewhere between unsweetened dark chocolate and astringent, not exactly what I would call pleasant, but not necessarily unpleasant either. The high is almost instantaneous and narcotic in nature, causing my eyes to redden, which is rare for me. I wouldn't want to smoke this herb all the time, but as an occasional nighttime fatty, it's a unique and potent treat. Grown outdoors organically in Humboldt, California.

The Black >>

Blockhead

Breeder Steve from Spice of Life Seeds cranks out yet another winner, Blockhead. This gorgeous strain was created by crossing a Sweet Tooth male (the same one used to make Sweet Tooth #3; see *Cannabible 2*, page 155) with a female known only as Product 19. Blockhead is extremely potent herb with a high that is strong and meditative, having the effect of making one quiet down and become more reflective. How very useful in today's crazy, stressed-out world! The plant, which when grown indoors can flower as long as nine weeks, puts out massive rock-hard nugs of gorgeous color. The smell is odd but desirable, a stinky sweetness bordering on sour. Two different versions are pictured, one grown outdoors in Northern California, and one grown indoors organically in soil.

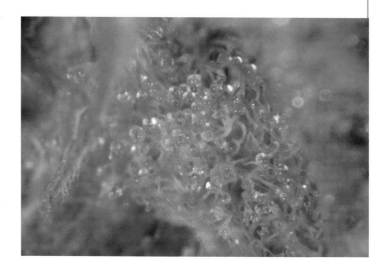

indoor organic soil

indoor organic soil

33

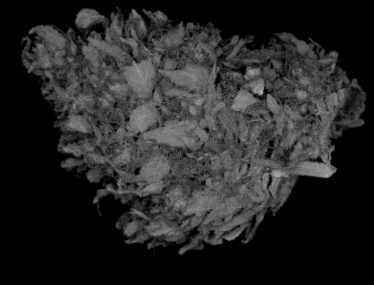

Blondie is a relatively rare, clone-only indica strain local to Northern California. When alive, the plant has a superpungent and skunky stench that's almost offensive. When dried, the finished product mellows somewhat in intensity but still has a nicely pungent and skunky flavor. The plants finish in late September and are moderate in yield. The high from Blondie is thick and penetrating, a bit disorienting perhaps. Grown outdoors organically in Mendocino, California.

Blondie

<< Blue Dot

This sativa-dominant strain is currently found in many of the cannabis buyers clubs in California. A medical grower in Sonoma, California developed it. As I understand the situation, it was originally called MGB, or Medical Grade Bud. Blue Dot originated in a club called the Pharmacy, where they sold it in gold tins with a blue dot, hence the name. The parents used to create her were White Widow, Skunk, Big Bud, and Northern Lights #5. I find the flavor of Blue Dot nothing spectacular, even boring compared to some of today's superstrains. The high, though rather strong, didn't pull me in any particular direction. I just felt very generically high.

CANNABIS ON THE WEB

Ever since the World Wide Web was popularized in the 1990s, the number of cannabis-related websites has exploded. As I write this, a Google search on the word *marijuana* brings up over 42,500,000 hits and the word *cannabis* brings up another 21,600,000. So many cannabis websites exist that it would be impossible to review them all, but I'd like to mention a few crucial ones. First and foremost is www.overgrow.com, without which the book in your hands would be less than it is. Overgrow is easily the best resource *ever* for cannabis lovers, plain and simple. Another of my favorites is www.cannabisworld.com, also a treasure trove of information for the herb lover in all of us. The forums contain millions of pages of text that discuss every aspect of ganja imaginable, from growing techniques to strain reports to advanced experiments and everything in between. Endless photos range in quality from terrible to nearly professional.

If you're looking for specific information and don't see the answer in the extensive FAQ sections of these websites, you can ask a question in one of the forums and often within minutes get answers from experts all over the world. Some members on these boards are absolutely brilliant and generously share their knowledge with the world. Of course, you'll also find some trolls: immature fools who show their lack of a clue at every chance possible. Many people, especially growers, stay away from these websites because they're paranoid about being watched by the authorities, but I don't think this should be of too much concern. At any given moment there are thousands of people cruising these boards, and the amount of manpower it would take to investigate all of them is impossibly high. Now, if you're growing five hundred plants, I don't recommend posting pictures of your garden—an unnecessary risk. But to cruise the forums, reading and learning, is a safe undertaking in my opinion. (I do it all the time!) It's sad that more growers don't use these vast resources, as they would benefit more than anyone, as would their ganja.

Another site worth checking out is www.420times.com. Lastly, a website I check every day is www.cannabisnews.com. This site provides links to news relating to cannabis/hemp every day, keeping the reader up-to-date on global cannabis happenings. Never before has a cannabis lover had such awesome access to other cannabis lovers on a worldwide scale, and this has had a great effect on today's cannabis scene. Thanks in part to these websites and their boards, the clone and seed trade has exploded, and top-quality genetics are more available than ever. Elite clones are much more available, too, though often still elusive. Growers are more educated, and better crops are being grown every day.

We owe a huge debt of gratitude to these boards, which are accessed for free, and any cannabis aficionado would be wise to check them out. If you would like to check them out but are still paranoid, consider moving to a state with legalized medical marijuana and getting a doctor's recommendation. Nothing is worth living in paranoia, as paranoia = stress = dis-ease. If nothing else, you could always use a public computer. It should also be mentioned that Jorge Cervantes, ganja guru and author of over a dozen grow books, is compiling *Overgrow: The Book*, sure to be a necessity in any ganjaphile's library. Oh yeah, and don't forget about www.thecannabible.com, too!

<< Blue Dream

Blue Dream is a Blueberry x Haze hybrid that's quickly gaining popularity in the Northern California medical herb scene. She's a clone-only strain known to produce bumper harvests of extremely high-quality herb. **Blue Dream** is a strong and resilient plant capable of pumping out well over two pounds per 1,000-watt light, making her a viable and desirable commercial strain. The live plants exhibit gorgeous purples and blues when the temperature drops, sometimes developing what looks like a neon effect. This batch was grown with chemicals hydroponically in a Sea of Green system and the flavor suffered as a result. No doubt the sweet blue and spicy flavor would have been much more powerful if the plants had been grown organically. The high from **Blue Dream** is clear and cerebral in nature, above average in strength, and sure to satisfy even a demanding connoisseur.

Blue Hen

Blue Hen is a hybrid from a company known as Bluegrass Seeds. They've crossed two proven winners—Blueberry and Super Silver Haze—to make this hybrid. You really can't go wrong with parents like these. I wish more "breeders" would go out and find interesting new genetics rather than just cross other seed companies' strains. But anything goes in the seed(y) game. Despite this, Blue Hen was wonderful smoke, fruity blue and spicy too, with great potency to boot. She seems to favor the indica side of her parentage, growing rock-hard nugs of glistening blueness and producing a heavy and lethargic buzz. This plant was grown outdoors in Mendocino, California.

<< Blue Satellite

The hybridization of Blue Satellite is a result of a collaboration of two of my favorite breeders on the planet: DJ Short and Breeder Steve from Spice of Life. The strain was developed in Switzerland by Steve, who created it by crossing a rare Blueberry sativa mother with a second generation Shishkeberry male. Shishkeberry is a wonderful cross of two fine Afghanis, known as "The Red and The Yellow," and a particularly awesome Blueberry male. When crossed back to DJ Short's Blueberry, the result is a wicked head-stash strain with a slightly astringent yet lovely fruity aroma, and a robust and interestingly fruity flavor. The effects of the Satellite are strong and heady, guaranteed to please any sativa (or indica!) lover. This batch was grown outdoors organically under the full California sun.

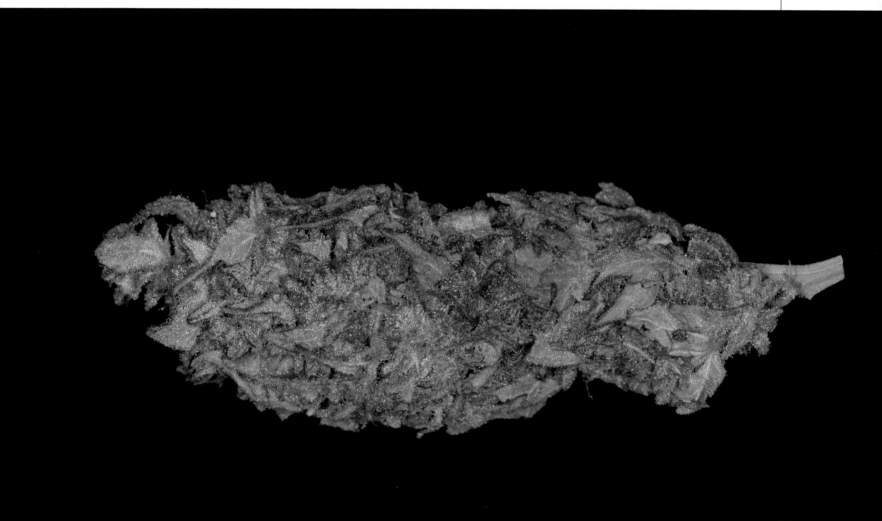

Blue Stupor >>

Northern California Growers Association (NCGA) crossed their tasty Blue Widow (*Cannabible 2*, page 32) with Stuporsonic, a strain from Sagamartha Seeds in Amsterdam. Stuporsonic is said to be a Swedish strain, believable due to its hemplike flavor and high. Blue Widow is NCGA's famous cross of DJ Short's Blueberry and a '98 Aloha Seeds White Widow. Luckily, this particular plant leaned toward the Blue Widow, evident by the luscious soft and blue flavor and the fact that it actually got me high. A fatty of this herb had an enticing flavor similar to that of mentholated blueberries. The high is strong and narcotic in nature, surely capable of leaving many partakers in a stupor. There is a warm body buzz to this one, suggesting good possibilities with pain relief. Grown outdoors in Mendocino, California.

<< stupersonic >>

41

Blueberry Sativa

This is a line of feminized seeds recently released by the Reeferman. It's a self-fertilized sativa phenotype of DJ Short's Blueberry circa '96. This herb has a lush and murky blue flavor, a deep fruity sativa punch that melts in your lungs. The plant is not a particularly heavy yielder, but it's not terrible either. It responds well to training and topping, and the end result is some very solid and lush nuggets. The high from Blueberry Sativa is fairly clear and up, and quite satisfying to this sativa lover. This expertly cultivated sample was grown indoors organically in a hydroponic setup and harvested after sixty-five days.

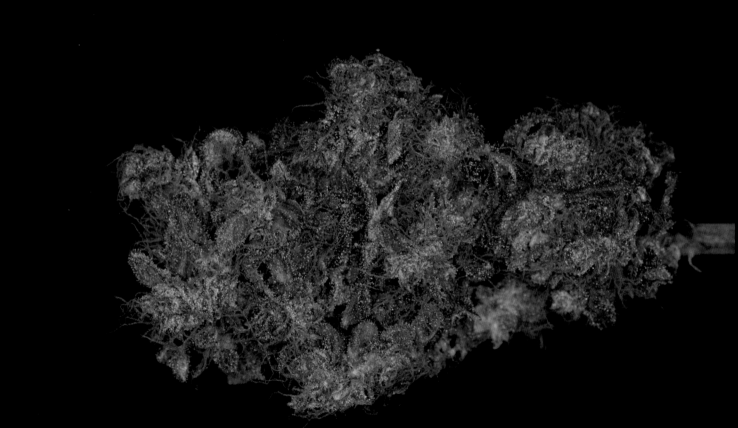

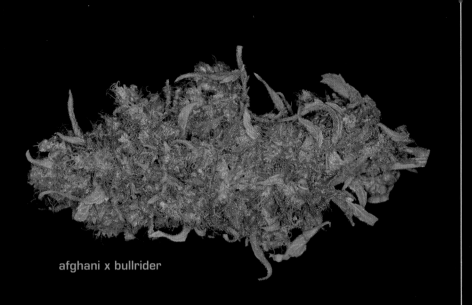

afghani x bullrider

big sur holy nug x holy gold

BRITISH COLUMBIA

After years of staying away from Canada due to a certain incident, I finally made it back out to B.C. for the harvest of 2004. (I was more than pleasantly surprised Canadian Customs actually let me in this time!) I was very impressed with the quality of herb that the connoisseurs in Canada were smoking (and vaporizing!). Exotic strains abound, as well as incredibly delicious local varieties. Every time a Canuck broke out some amazing herb, I felt the need to ask, "How come you guys never send *this* stuff down to the states?" (Seems like everyone in the United States knows that the B.C. export product—unlovingly referred to as "Beasters"—is garbage.) Invariably, the response I got every time was "Because we keep the good stuff to smoke, eh!" To which I would reply, "Why not only grow good stuff?" The reality of the situation, I've learned, is that plenty of great B.C. herb makes its way to the States, but it's not sold as B.C. Doing so would lower the value by about $1,500 per pound or more. So instead it's called "Humboldt" or "Seattle" or basically anything other than Beasters. Look for the good organic B.C. herb grown outdoors; you will be pleased!

This spread represents some of the better nugs I found while on the trip. Others are explored in fuller detail in other parts of this book.

sweet pea

kandahar afghani

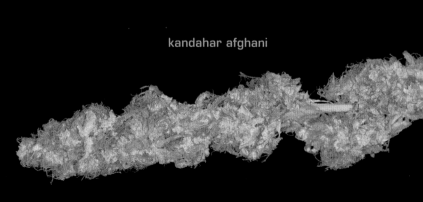

44

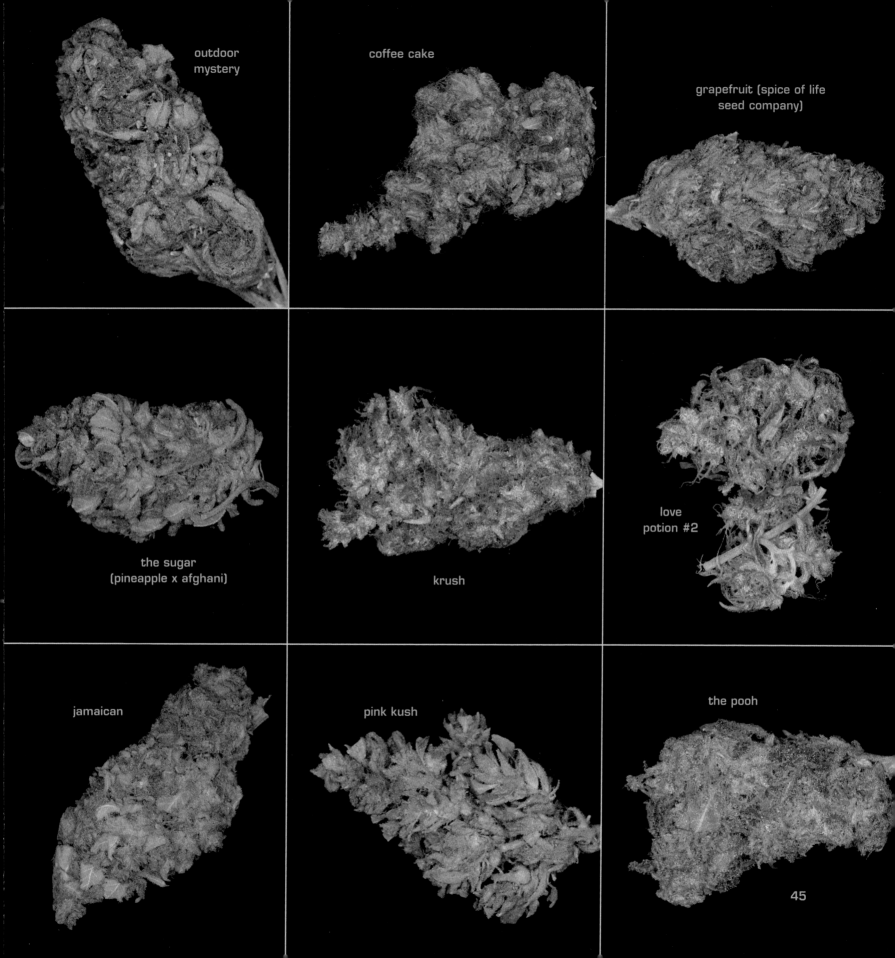

outdoor mystery

coffee cake

grapefruit (spice of life seed company)

the sugar (pineapple x afghani)

krush

love potion #2

jamaican

pink kush

the pooh

45

BEASTERS

I have spoken with people on all sides of the issue known as "Beasters," which is what Americans call the mass-produced, warehouse-grown, chemically fed schwag that British Columbia exports to the United States by the ton. The funny thing is, when you bring this up to Canadians, they act as if they don't know what you're talking about. They respond with "We don't ever see that" or "The good stuff stays in Canada."

Beasters. I wouldn't be surprised if it was the most-often-smoked herb in the United States—I see it everywhere I go. Its effects on the American cannabis scene are numerous and far-reaching. Picture, if you will, some of these implications and thoughts:

- The entire pricing structure of cannabis in the United States has been turned upside down to the point where, in most places, only select clones get top dollar. As one example, old-school organic outdoor West Coast growers have had to lower their prices by $1,500 a pound to compete with Beasters, even though their product is of much higher quality.

- Uninformed American smokers buy Beasters because they think it looks great; they're fooled by the white appearance and think that it's actually very resinous. (Sparkly resin glands are what get you high, not the white stalks so prevalent on most Beasters.)

- Buyers go to Canada to pick up loads, and they buy Beasters because they think that's what people want. Plus, it's by far the most available herb.

- Skilled outdoor organic growers in British Columbia have given up, gotten regular jobs, and no longer even grow outdoors because none of the buyers seem to want outdoor herb anymore, and if they do, it's only at a patheti-

cally low price. Others have just jumped on the bandwagon and started growing chemmy indoor herb.

- Dealers who are connoisseurs buy Beasters dirt cheap, knowing that it's garbage and never smoking a single hit, just to make money. "It's just work," they rationalize.

- There are sixteen-year-old kids in Alabama who could identify Beasters blindfolded and are totally sick of it, but it's all they can get most of the time.

- Legitimate medical marijuana patients have gotten sick(er) from smoking Beasters because it's loaded with chemicals—nasty fertilizer salts—that were never flushed.

This is a plea to all cannabis smokers, buyers, growers, smugglers, and dealers: *Please, no more Beasters! Please stop growing this stuff! Please stop sending this stuff! Please stop buying this stuff! Please stop supporting this stuff! We will gladly pay more for organic herb!*

Next time your supplier offers Beasters, just say know! How many times do you think that would have to happen before things started changing? Before the *love* started coming around again? It's the law of supply and demand. If we demand better herb, it will be supplied.

Every time you buy Beasters, you're sending a message to the growers, buyers, and smugglers: We will buy your chemmy Beasters. (It's the same with anything you support with your money, really.)

At this point you may be wondering, why do Beasters suck? Read "Why Most Pot Sucks," on page 145. Your typical Beasters have broken every rule on the list. Plus, the strains commonly grown are chosen strictly for yield, not quality of flavor or high—not to mention that large portions of Beasters are

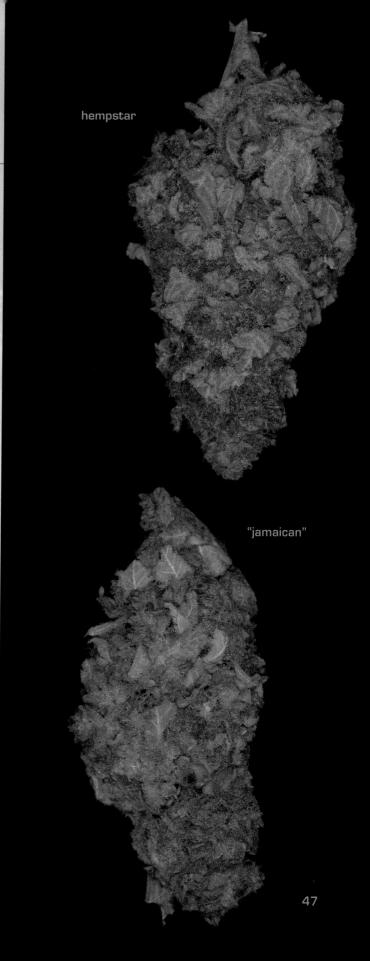

hempstar

"jamaican"

"kiefed," bounced on screens to remove resin glands. (Which *they* keep!)

Another thing to consider is that Beasters are mostly grown by organizations with one thing in mind—money. This shows clearly in their end product. Beasters is the Wal-Mart of cannabis: really cheap and really low quality. Organic herb, on the other hand, whether grown indoors or outdoors, is normally produced by people who take pride in growing the finest ganja possible. Who do you want to support? You wield much power with your spending dollar. Personally, I want to support the small, organic family farmers.

As we approach the end of the era of cheap fossil fuels, which power the lights that grow all this indoor bud (and also supply the petroleum-based chemical fertilizers), it is especially important that enlightened (pardon the pun) cannabis growers go back to their roots and relearn how to grow their crops outdoors and organically, even biodynamically. (Biodynamic farming is an invention of Rudolph Steiner that utilizes cosmic forces and special handmade preparations that are highly beneficial to plants and soil.)

Just say No to Beasters! And if you are a commercial Beasters grower, please, on behalf of all of us, at least switch to organic hydroponics! I highly recommend Botanicare's line of products. Just try it—the resulting cannabis tastes so much better! I know you will be pleased!

I want to again mention that there are incredible organic farmers in B.C., though their product is by far the minority, at least in terms of what's exported to the United States, and not what I would call Beasters. These high-quality nugs are usually sold as U.S.-grown herb, given that if they're identified as B.C. product, the value goes down substantially.

I have even seen a T-shirt that says, "Friends don't let friends smoke Beasters!"

Hempstar and "Jamaican" are the two most common commercial Beasters strains. To the untrained eye, they look great. And if they were consciously and organically grown, they would have been decent. Notice the lack of sparkly resin glands.

Bronze Berry

Bronze Berry is a relatively rare strain. I've heard of only a few people growing it. It was created by an Australian breeder named Rodwal, who blended Dutch Passion's Orange Bud and DJ Short's Blueberry (*Cannabible 1*, page 44) with a mutant Cali-O indica cross known as Bronze Whaler. The end result is a gorgeous plant with extreme resin production and a lovely amaretto scent when flowering. The flavor of this multihybrid is spicy orange berry, though to be honest, due to the chemical fertilizers used, I don't feel I can write a fair flavor description because I know the herb would have tasted so much better if grown organically. The high from **Bronze Berry** is strong and cloudy, heavily indica based, and left me craving a nice sativa.

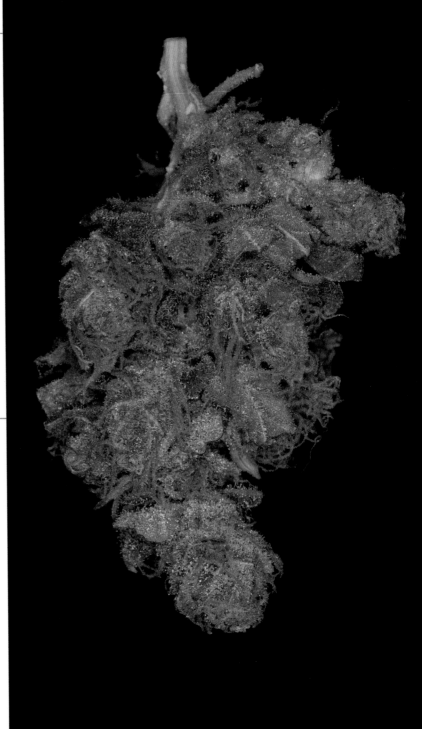

Bubba Kush >>

This highly sought-after West Coast indica-dominant clone is finally becoming more available, thank the Goddess! Bubba Kush, I'm told, was created by crossing the old-school Bubblegum clone with a Master Kush male. Apparently there are two or three different versions going around: the pure Bubba Kush as well as crosses made in order to increase the yield. Most people are growing the cross, though they are unaware of it. The pure Bubba Kush is a very small plant. In a garden of plants all sown at the same time, she will be by far the smallest. She simply will not get large! The flavor of this exquisite herb is among the best out there. It's very complex, a fizzy and pungent blend of lemon-lime soap and a crazy outer-space spiciness that is quite different from the haze spiciness many of us know and love. It leaves an incredible skunky aftertaste in your mouth for what seems like weeks. The high is devastatingly strong and turned me into a red-eyed happy retard almost instantly. This herb will get you very high regardless of tolerance. That alone makes it very special medicine. If you can find the real deal, get it—no matter what it costs! This sample was grown outdoors organically in Northern California.

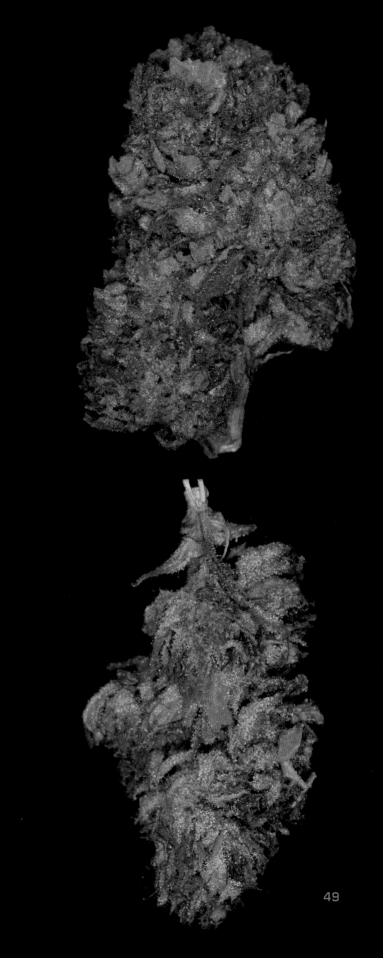

<< Bubba Kush

50

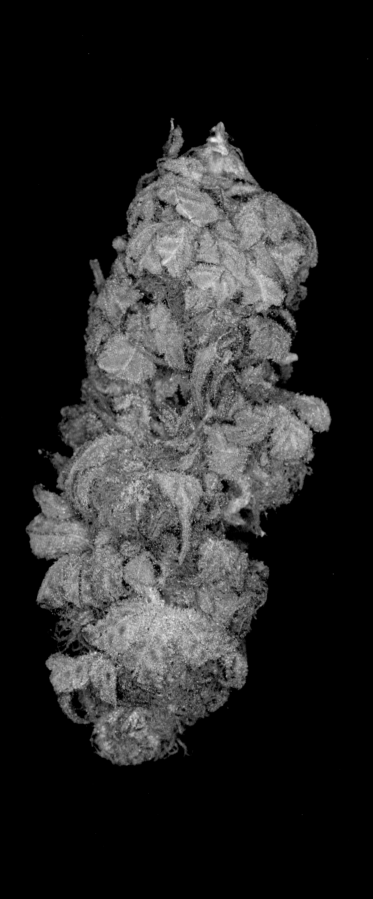

Bubblegun

This hybridized cross of Sensi Seeds Bubblegum and Serious Seeds AK47 has been appearing more and more on the connoisseur circuit lately, earning it a spot in the third Canna-bible. The fact that it smells so good didn't hurt its chances either. I really look forward to the invention of the "smell camera"! Bubblegun is indeed a vigorous hybrid, successfully high-lighting the intense candied sweet-ness of Bubblegum while taking on the massive size and yield of AK47. This sample was grown indoors organically in soil. The clone of this phenotype is quickly making its way around the West Coast.

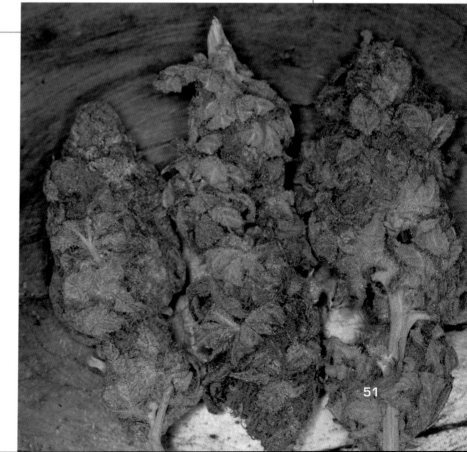

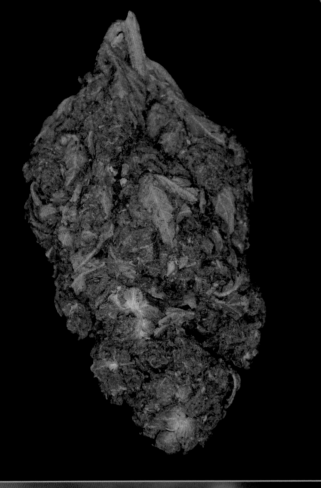

Burmese x Fuckin Incredible

From Vancouver Island Seed Company we have Burmese x Fuckin Incredible. A pack of seeds shows two major phenotypes, one indica dominant and one sativa dominant. Hermaphrodites are not uncommon with this strain, and many others from this company. The Burmese is a popular clone in Vancouver. Said to be a pure landrace sativa from Burma, it seems to me to have some indica crossed into it. No one seems to know what Fuckin Incredible is. This bud gave me an agitated and grungy high that I did not like. Some have reported getting good phenotypes from this cross, though they all had slight hermaphrodite problems. The flowering time is around sixty-three days indoors, while outdoors it will finish in mid-September. This sample was grown indoors organically in soil.

Bwanana >>

This relatively rare strain has been steadily gaining popularity in recent years. I have been told that she's a cross of Sweet Skunk x Maui Haze, and I have no reason not to believe it. The plant is definitely mostly a sativa, evident by her lanky structure and thin-bladed leaves. The herb has a lovely flowery and fruity fragrance, though I must say that on the two different batches I sampled, the aroma didn't transition to flavor very well, making for a rather bland smoke. The high, however, is no letdown. It's a very up and positive high, the kind I prefer. But to me, flavor is the most important factor, so I am no huge fan of Bwanana.

indoor organic

53

"COMPASSIONATE" IND PROGRAM— ULTIMATE HYPOCRISY!

An incredible hypocrisy is festering in the medical marijuana community. Did you know that despite the fact that the federal government claims marijuana has no medicinal value and it is too dangerous to be used as medicine, they have been supplying it to seven patients every month since the 1970s? And did you know that those patients have greatly benefited from that marijuana, with no adverse effects on their health? What I'm talking about is the federal Compassionate Investigative New Drug (IND) program.

It all started in 1976, when a glaucoma patient named Robert Randall employed the rarely used common law doctrine of necessity to defend himself against criminal charges of growing marijuana. In this landmark case, *U.S. v. Randall*, federal judge James Washington ruled in favor of Randall, agreeing that his use of the healing herb was in fact a medical necessity. In May 1976, federal agencies began providing Randall with licit, FDA-approved medical marijuana, grown at the University of Mississippi at the government research farm. Randall was far from silent about his victory, which led to another case, *Randall v. U.S.* What happened was that the government tried to silence Randall by ending his legal access to marijuana, so in response he sued the FDA, the DEA, the National Institute on Drug Abuse, the Department of Justice, and the Department of Health, Education, and Welfare. The day after the suit was filed, the federal government requested a (quiet) out-of-court settlement, in which Randall was provided with prescriptive access to marijuana through a federal pharmacy near his home. The settlement in *Randall v. U.S.* became the legal basis for the FDA's Compassionate IND program.

In the beginning, the program was limited to patients afflicted with marijuana-responsive disorders, as well as some orphan drugs (drugs not marketed because limited use makes them unprofitable). But in the 1980s, the program was expanded to include HIV-positive patients seeking legal access to drugs that had not yet received FDA approval, and soon after, more patients joined the program. In spite of the incidence of AIDS skyrocketing and the need for medical marijuana growing fast, the uncompassionate George H. W. Bush administration decided to shut the program down in 1991. Too many people were asking for medical marijuana, and in order for marijuana to be classified as a prohibited schedule I drug, it can't have "accepted medical use in treatment" in the United States. The feds knew that approving thousands of people into the Compassionate IND program would undermine that criteria and that marijuana would have to be rescheduled, which they had no intention of doing. So instead, in a completely uncompassionate move, they ended the program.

The lucky but few existing patients were grandfathered in because the government knew that publicly embarrassing court cases would be required to deny them medicine. At the time of this writing, seven of those patients are still alive, still smoking the government's schwag. It's grown from Mexican seeds, then rolled and packaged at the Research Triangle Institute in North Carolina under the supervision of the National Institute on Drug Abuse (NIDA). It's mostly leaves and stems and has very low levels of THC. The patients have no other contact with the federal government. There's no ID card or official paperwork, only some decades-old letters and pharmacy phone numbers. The patients are often harassed or detained: A phone call to a certain informed person at the DEA is necessary to straighten things out from time to time. On December 1, 1999, the

Clinton administration announced that the IND program would not be reopened.

Recent polls indicate that 70 to 80 percent of the American public approves of the use of medical marijuana by the general population. Yet when decriminalization advocates push for reform, the government claims there simply isn't enough research to warrant the reclassification of a potentially dangerous drug. The call for evidence operates in a vicious cycle, as the drug laws themselves have stood in the way of the very same research they require. U.S. scientists who seek to perform controlled studies on cannabis face an impossible bureaucratic red tape scenario. To make matters even worse, officials have repeatedly ignored the findings of their own commissioned research panels, which have proven again and again that marijuana is a safe substance that has many medical applications.

Irvin Rosenfeld, one of the remaining recipients of medical marijuana under the Compassionate IND program, notes that the federal government has had ample opportunity to do a full-scale study on long-term controlled use of medical marijuana, but they aren't interested. *They don't even want to know.* All the talk about not having sufficient evidence, about not having controlled scientific studies—total bullshit. Rosenfeld, who has been smoking ten to twelve federal joints a day for well over twenty years, and some other patients got involved in their own study. They received MRI brain scans, pulmonary function tests, chest X-rays, neuropsychological tests, hormone and immunological assays, electroencephalography (brain wave recording), and clinical neurological examinations. The results showed that, other than the original condition for which they were using marijuana, there was nothing wrong with them—no significant adverse affects from smoking ten to twelve joints a day. Rosenfeld even had 108 percent lung capacity; that's after smoking marijuana for over thirty years, twenty-two years under the IND program—that's over eighty thousand federal joints.

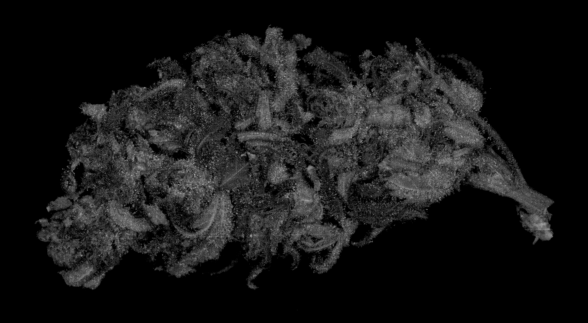

Homegrown Fantaseeds in Amsterdam has released Caramella, named for its unique caramel-maple aroma. Yes, it's a stretch, but if I close my eyes I can sort of smell caramel. Caramella is an indica-sativa hybrid that's been bred for fifteen years in Holland and is selected for taste and a high calyx-to-leaf ratio. The plant may do well in Holland, but every time I see it on the West Coast it's sickly and infested with just about everything imaginable. The high was moderately strong at best. Grown outdoors in Humboldt, California.

Caramella

Champagne

Champagne is a Hash Plant variety that was a big part of the B.C. commercial herb scene in the 1990s. It's much less common today, though you can still find it from time to time. She was most likely bred from the amazing Kush strains in Vancouver, including the King and Pink lines. Champagne is a heavy-yielding strain with a powerful narcotic buzz. If you like powerful indicas, this one might be for you. The flavor of Champagne is pleasant and actually touches on the flavors of real champagne—fizzy and slightly astringent. Though the flavor isn't overwhelming, it's not what I would call bland either. The samples I got were hydroponically grown with chemicals, which definitely had a negative effect on the overall flavor and smoking experience. Organic growing really is the only method of cultivation that allows the full flavor of a strain to be experienced. Special thanks to the brother who drove this freshly harvested cola across New York to submit it for *Cannabible 3*. You rock!

57

Cosmic Blue is an astoundingly quick Blueberry hybrid from a company called Good Gear Seeds. They crossed their version of Blueberry, called Black Goo, with Wonder (see *Cannabible 2*, page 175) and selected repeatedly for early harvest. The project was apparently successful, as the bud shown was harvested in only thirty-eight days in a greenhouse. Even more astounding is that the plant can be grown in 70 percent shade and still produce dense nuggets. There are two phenotypes: an early one and a late one. The flavor is mildly sweet and blue, and not overwhelming by any means.

Cosmic
Blue >>

PRAISES TO THE POT DEALER

So often in modern society dealers of cannabis flowers are demonized and vilified, sometimes even put in cages, for passing on a medicine that has been safely used and enjoyed for millennia. How sad, indeed. I believe society should praise cannabis dealers for their work, at least the ones with a sense of morality. Consider this: Retail stores selling legal and often vibration-lowering products make an average of 100 percent profit on the items they sell, and sometimes up to 300 percent profit or more. Their products are legal, so they don't face the dangers of prison or robberies like a cannabis retailer too often does. But the average cannabis dealer makes only 10 to 20 percent profit on what they sell, despite the huge risks and investments inherent in the business. And the product they sell is healing and raises a person's vibration. So, if you have a good dealer, smoke them out and tell them you love them more often. They're taking a big risk for you and making a lot less than Wal-Mart!

Cotton Candy x Romulan

Federation Seed Company's Cotton Candy is actually a knockoff of Sweet Tooth (see *Cannabible 2*, page 155) from Spice of Life. More seediness in the seed business. Nevertheless, it's a great strain, and when crossed with a Romulan (see *Cannabible 1*, page 57) male, it produced a hybrid of extreme greatness. (Actually, the male must have been a Romulan hybrid, as in its pure form Romulan is a female clone.) I picked up this nug at a cannabis buyers club in San Francisco. It was the best they had out of over forty strains, in my opinion and that of the salesman. The flavor is extremely sweet, hitting on tropical punch and Skittles, with a skunky base to bring it on home. The high was very heady and narcotic feeling, even sleepy at times. This sample was grown indoors organically in soil.

<< moldy >>

Dalat

There's been a lot of talk about Dalat on the cannabis boards. The strain is a landrace from Vietnam, where a French family has lovingly grown it for generations. These plants grow over twenty feet tall in their native environment. In order to get these monsters to grow indoors, they must be repeatedly tied down and topped. The flowering time on Dalat is an astonishing four to five months. If you can wait that long, the harvest size is fairly large. Interestingly, when grown indoors Dalat loses its shade leaves, growing with only single-bladed leaves. Unfortunately, all the samples I got of Dalat had mold, which basically ruined the herb. Several attempts were made to save the plant, but to no avail. To me, this plant is screaming, "I want to be outside!" The man who deliverd the Dalat describes the odor as "dead meat and sativa." Scary.

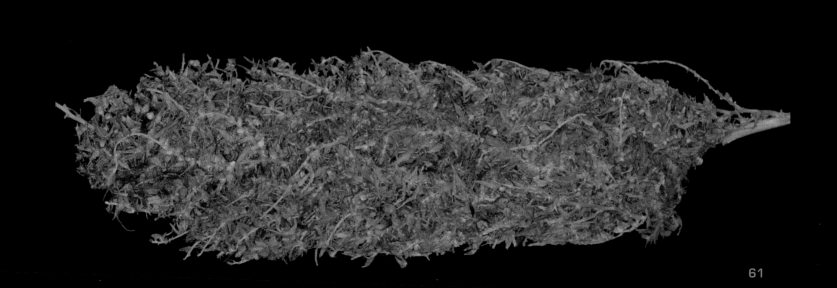

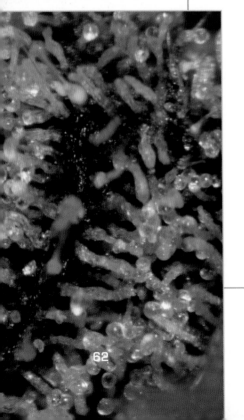

This stunning pure indica is a Tom Hill strain that goes by many a name. Originally from Afghanistan, Deep Chunk has been in Northern California for over thirty years, where it has been heavily inbred and reworked by Mr. Hill. Selections were made for flavor and potency, both of which are awesome in the finished product. Deep Chunk grows extraordinarily fat leaves with gorgeous dark green coloring. The flowers often turn purple late in the season. Though the yield is low, this headstash strain pumps out insane amounts of resin and has a pungent flavor that screams hash, pine, and skunk, with a thick Kushy bottom end. The high is extremely strong, numbing at times, floaty at others. This is very heavy stuff, and highly medicinal as well. When grown outdoors, the plants finish in late September to early October. Indoors, expect flowering to take just under sixty days. The dried bud pictured was grown indoors organically in soil. The live plants shown are known as Monkey Balls and were grown outdoors organically in Northern California. I was told they were the same strain, but I have my doubts.

Deep Chunk, aka Monkey Balls, aka Hindu Death Cabbage

Diesel

diesel: Grown outdoors in Maui. This is what herb looks like in heaven!

BREAKDOWN

I write this in the hope of clearing up the mass confusion surrounding the Diesel lineage. I've gotten the real story from the actual folks responsible for Diesel, so here goes: Diesel comes from a seed that was found in a bag of the insanely delicious Colorado indica known as Chem/Dawg (see *Cannabible 2*, page 46). Two friends met on a Dead tour in '91 (thank you Jerry!), and a pound containing twelve seeds of the majestic Chem/Dawg, whose lineage is still somewhat of a mystery, made its way to Massachusetts. As for the father of those seeds, this is also somewhat of a mystery. This much is known: The person who had the Chem/Dawg in Colorado grew only Chem/Dawg, so it was probably a Chem/Dawg male or hermaphrodite that fathered the seeds. The seeds found in this legendary bag of herb were grown, and from them came some truly phenomenal ganja. At this point, another good friend was met on a Phish tour (thanks boys!), and clones of this awesome Chem/Dawg offspring passed on to this lucky new friend. The new grower from New York City, didn't like the name Chem/Dawg so he started calling it Diesel. This is the Diesel that some of us are lucky enough to know and love.

A couple of years later, a Super Skunk x Sensi Northern Lights was crossed with the newly named Diesel and thus was created Headband (pictured, page 66), Daywrecker Diesel, and Diesel #1 (see *Cannabible 1*, page 65). Soon after that, a hermaphroditic Massachusetts Super Skunk pollinated the Diesel, and from the seeds it created, Sour Diesel was born. Then there's OG Kush (page 152), which is a sister to Sour Diesel. The original Massachusetts Chem/Dawg family has made several newer crosses, and they are featured here. Lastly, for good reason, I'll mention Soma's NYCD Diesel, which barely, if at all, resembles the real Diesel. It has a more citrusy flavor and is much weaker than the real Diesel. The thing that I love so much about the real Diesel and its hybrids is their aftertaste. Don't get me wrong, the exhalation is almost orgasmic, but it's after the smoke stops coming out that you notice this sour kind of fuel flavor that just coats your entire mouth and throat. It's freakin' outrageous. I would smoke it even if it didn't have THC, which by the way, it has massive amounts.

The lesson learned here is that we should all be very thankful to the Grateful Dead and Phish not only for their awesome music but for all the great connections that were made on tour.

(clockwise from top left)

bubblechem: Bubbleberry x Chem/Dawg Sister. From the Massachusetts Chem/Dawg family, grown indoors organically in soil.

chem/dawg d: From another seed found in the batch of original seed—started in 2000. Only a few people have this one. From the Massachusetts Chem/Dawg family, grown indoors organically in soil.

chem/dawg sister: From another seed from the original Chem/Dawg line, much less circulated—started in '96. Only a few people have this one. From the Massachusetts Chem/Dawg family, grown indoors organically in soil.

massachusetts super skunk: This is the one used to create Sour Diesel. Mega-roadkill, almost offensive! Nothing like the boring, sweet Dutch Super Skunk. From the Massachusetts Chem/Dawg family, grown indoors organically in soil.

supersnowdawg: Snow x Skunk x BubbleChem: Tastes like candy! From the Massachusetts Chem/Dawg family, grown indoors organically in soil.

superdawg, aka orange giesel: Super Skunk x Chem/Dawg D. Words cannot describe. From the Massachusetts Chem/Dawg family, grown indoors organically in soil.

lemon diesel: Grown in Oregon. Fantastic!

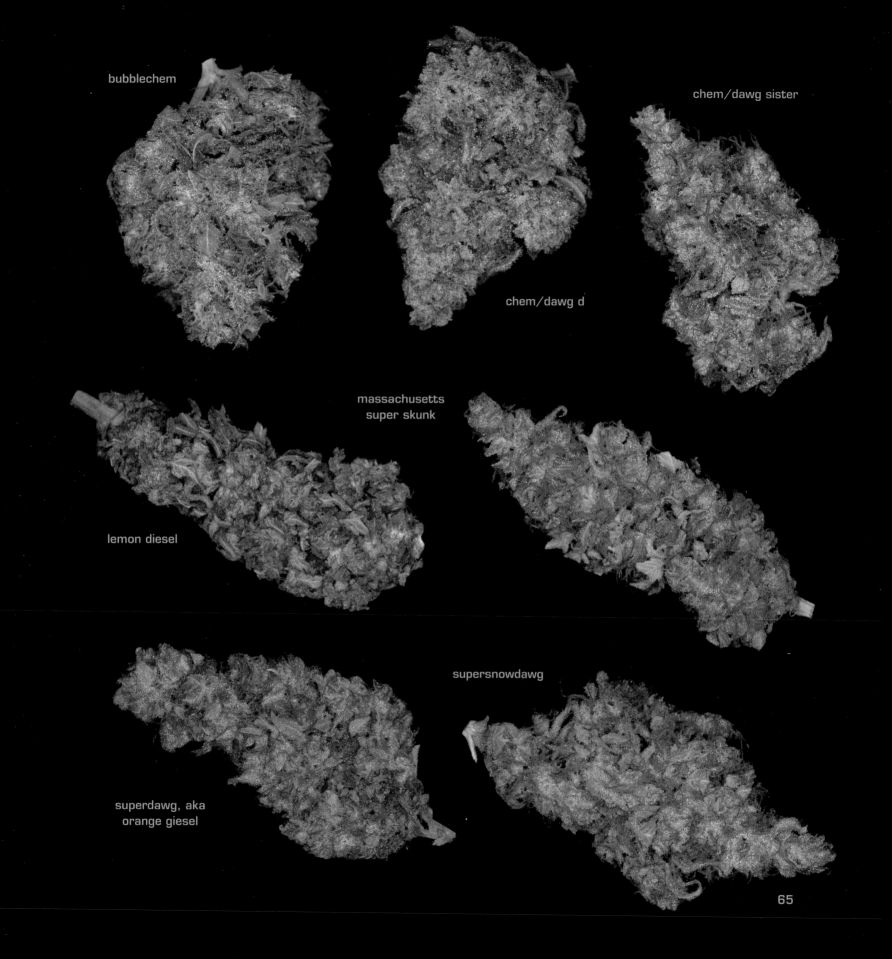

bubblechem

chem/dawg sister

chem/dawg d

massachusetts
super skunk

lemon diesel

supersnowdawg

superdawg, aka
orange giesel

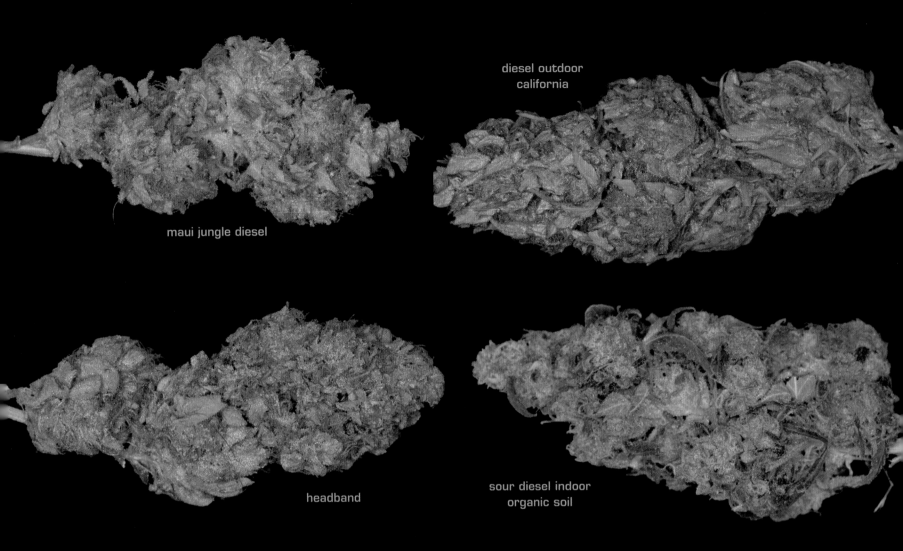

diesel outdoor
california

maui jungle diesel

headband

sour diesel indoor
organic soil

Diesel

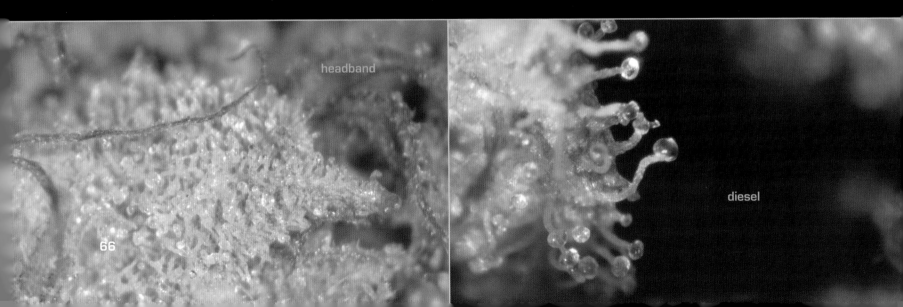

headband

diesel

66

(opposite: clockwise from top left)

diesel (dried): Grown outdoors organically in the jungles of Maui.

sour diesel: Grown outdoors in California.

sour diesel: Superstrong and superpotent. Grown indoors organically in soil.

headband: (Super Skunk x Northern Lights) x Diesel.

sour diesel: grown outdoors in mendocino, california

headband live

Diesel

berryjuana
organic soil

cannalope haze
organic hydro

cannalope haze
organic soil

blueberry
haze

serial killer
organic soil

sharksbreath
organic hydro

la confidential
organic hydro

rocklock
organic soil

68

<< DNA Genetics

DNA is a relatively new seed company on the Dutch scene. It's comprised of some American expats from the Southern California area, home to some of the most incredible cannabis genetics on the planet. They have brought some of these amazing strains to Amsterdam, where they're breeding them for seed sales. They've already won several Cannabis Cups and awards, including first place in the sativa category with Martian Mean Green and second place in the indica cup with LA Confidential, and that was just at the 2005 Cannabis Cup! I photographed these lovely nuggets while at the Cannabis Cup in 2004, when I met DNA for the first time. They kindly supplied me with these sweet samples, which I liked very much.

The ones that stood out the most were LA Confidential and Rocklock. They don't want to release the lineage on LA Confidential but I taste Bubba Kush in there somewhere. LA Confidential has a deep, rich, fruity, and slightly spicy aroma that fully comes through in the smoke. The high? Intense and trippy! Also very impressive was Rocklock (Rockstar x Warlock). It has one of the sweetest aromas I've ever experienced. When a bud is ground, it lets off an intensely sweet aroma similar to concentrated Kool-Aid or perhaps a hot, sucked-on candy. This artificial, candylike sweetness did not all transition to taste; the flavor of the smoke is more your standard sweetness. The high is strong, but it takes a while to really hit you—a creeper for sure.

I also really liked the Cannalope Haze (Haze Brothers x Michoacán Mexican Sativa). This beautiful sativa strain has a lovely and pronounced melon flavor, sweet and delicious for sure. The flowering time is exceptionally low for a Haze hybrid, a respectable eight weeks. Cannalope Haze has already won awards at the International Cannagraphic 420 Grower's Cup in Holland. I expect to see it gain popularity. Also pictured are Berryjuana (Herijuana x Blueberry Sativa), Blueberry Haze (DJ Short's Blueberry x Dutch Haze), Serial Killer (Cali Grapefruit x Mexican sativa), and lastly, Sharksbreath (Great White Shark x Jamaican Lambs Bread).

Kudos to DNA for bringing some fresh genetics to Amsterdam!

Donkey
Dick >>

There are two different seed companies selling a strain called Donkey Dick, West Coast Seed Co., and Mighty Mite Seeds. The two definitely seem related. Donkey Dick is a commercial Skunk strain, famous for producing long, phallic colas. Nothing superexotic here, just a nice fat Skunk selection with a typical Skunk flavor and a typical Skunk high. Yawn.

Magus Genetics in Amsterdam, a relatively new company, takes the credit for this indica-dominant hybrid. They made it by crossing a pre-2000 Chronic (see *Cannabible 1*, page 60) female with a Warlock (see *Cannabible 1*, page 179) male. The resultant hybrid appears to lean toward the indica side of the spectrum, though if grown right it produces huge, sativa-like buds. Most plants produce multiple large colas, which often must be supported to prevent them from snapping under their own girth. Double Dutch has a lovely floral aroma, hinting at wildflowers and sweet candy. The high is quite strong, a bit dreamy perhaps, which isn't surprising considering the highly potent parental material used. She's usually ready to harvest around sixty days into flowering.

Double Dutch

FOUR CANNABIS SPECIES

In the book *Hemp Diseases and Pests*, by McPartland, Clark, and Watson, cannabis is broken into four species instead of the three most people know of:

1. *Cannabis sativa*: over three meters tall.

2. *Cannabis indica*: one and a half to three meters tall.

3. *Cannabis afghanica*: under one and a half meters tall.

4. *Cannabis ruderalis*: half a meter tall and autoflowering.

Indicas are often confused with sativas, and afghanicas are often mistakenly called indicas. True indicas come from India, while, predictably, the real afghanicas are from Afghanistan. The region in between India and Afghanistan is the Hindu Kush mountain range, and the "Kushes" that most people grow are probably hybrids of indicas and afghanicas. True indicas often can be found hiding within Kush genetics—they stretch and they have thin leaves, thin stems, small nuggets, and that brilliant Kush flavor. The afghanica-dominant plants are very small and have fat leaves, fat stems, and fat, greasy nuggets. If what McPartland, Clark, and Watson say is true, and they are very smart, then a reclassification of many of today's strains might be in order.

FLOWER ESSENCES

I'm sure many of you have heard of Bach flower essences. For those of you who haven't, I'll explain the basics. First off, flower essences are not essential oils. They are two completely different things. Flower essences are part of an ancient wisdom and have been used by aboriginal cultures throughout the world for millennia. Paracelsus, a sixteenth-century master physician and herbalist, used essences, but they were truly reinvented and popularized in the 1930s by an English physician, Dr. Edward Bach. Bach, who was highly sensitive and had a keen interest in homeopathy, closely observed the varying emotional and mental states of various people. Then, after observing the same states in himself, he was able to find flower essences to serve as remedies for various conditions. He characterized the effects different essences could have on emotions and found that if he administered the right flower essence to decrease a prevailing emotion, physical ailments, too, could also be healed. He then developed the Bach flower remedies, which are still popular throughout the world.

In the most basic sense, essences are vibrational energy patterns stored in pure water. It is important to note that water is a living entity with a memory and an ability to hold vibrational information. Flower essences are water-based solutions that contain the vibrational energies of flowers. They're made by floating mature flowers (or sometimes other plant parts, gems, and so on) in springwater for a certain amount of time, allowing the light of the sun, and in some cases the moon and stars, to help the water absorb the vibrational energy signature of the flowers. This creates what is known as the "mother essence," which is then diluted and kept in a liquid medium (generally water with a preservative like brandy added). This process is a real art form. The intent and the awareness of the person making the flower essence are of crucial importance and cannot be underestimated. A few drops of the finished product, which contains virtually no plant matter, are placed under the tongue. Simple as that.

In the words of Dr. Bach, flower essences "cure by flooding our bodies with beautiful vibrations of Higher Nature which melt dis-ease like snow in the sunshine." Flower essences fill our energetic bodies with the vibrations they contain while at the same time helping to loosen any energetic blockages that prevent us from vibrating at our highest natural frequency. This may sound like hippie folklore to some, but flower essences are an accepted natural medicine and healing modality around the world. There are millions of people who attest to their effectiveness for a wide range of conditions, be they physical, mental, emotional, or spiritual.

Personally, I always carry a bottle of Bach Rescue Remedy when traveling. It amazes me how well (and quickly) it calms me when the seemingly unavoidable stress of travel hits. Currently, flower essences are primarily used for treating humans and sometimes pets. However, the implications of all this for growers of cannabis are many. First off, there's the possibility of creating flower essences from cannabis flowers, for treating not only humans but perhaps even other cannabis plants. As far as I know, there's no information about this form of cannabis vibrational medicine in the current literature, so I'm charting new territory. A friend and I made two different cannabis flower essences: an indica and a sativa, Purps and Mothership respectively. Further testing will be done as time permits. (For those who are inevitably wondering, they contain no THC and don't get you high. Okay, maybe they do make your vibration higher!) There is also the possibility of treating cannabis plants with flower essences from *other* plants. Currently a handful of highly advanced farmers (noncannabis, as far as I know) use flower essences to treat their crops. Here are some of the flower essences most commonly used to treat plants:

- **Aloe Vera**: Good for hot weather conditions; helps plants stay cool and hold their energy.

- **Cayenne**: Great for cuttings and rootlets; helps produce fine rootlet hairs quickly. Improves growth speed when combined with tansy.

- **Corn**: For plants grown in pots that are off the ground, especially those in high-rise buildings; helps them connect to the earth's energies.

- **Mulla Mulla**: Beneficial in really hot weather.

- **Rescue Remedy**: Use for stress, trauma, or shock (transplanting, pruning).

- **Self-Heal**: Beneficial when pruning and also for sick plants; good when combined with yarrow and thyme.

- **She Oak**: Useful with seeds that may be old, as it helps with fertility.

- **Sunflower**: Useful for plants that don't get enough sunlight.

- **Sweet Pea**: For plants that are grown in crowded areas or situations, especially when a new plant is introduced to an area where plants are already established; helps plants get along well together.

- **Tansy**: Great when transplanting; gives plants energy and vitality.

- **Walnut**: Helps with transition (transplanting, moving).

All of these benefits would surely apply to the cultivation of cannabis. I write this in the hopes that some of the highly advanced (and highly sensitive) growers of organic cannabis will do their own experiments and

pass the information on (www.overgrow.com would be a great place to share) so that these vibrational gifts from nature can be utilized in the broadest way. I say organic growers only because chemicals would immediately destroy the essence, which is what they eventually do to everything they come into contact with. Use of flower essences and other esoteric methods could very well be the next steps to producing the highest-quality cannabis flowers imaginable.

73

outdoor maui

What do you get when you cross arguably two of the most flavorful strains on the planet? Some insanely tasty herb. A self-fertilized Diesel plant was crossed with the legendary HP13, and the result is nothing less than spectacular. This hybrid was created in 2004, so not many people have it yet. Hopefully this will change soon. Diesel and HP13 are probably the two most expensive and sought-after strains in the thriving NYC ganja trade (and in many other places as well), so don't expect this herb to come cheap. The flavor touches on the full gamut of possibilities, from hashy to roadkill skunky, not to mention intense fruit and salty garlic. As you might expect, the high of this herb is powerful and heavy. It gave me intense head rushes when I stood up; I often wondered if I would pass out. It never happened, but it certainly came close!

DP >>

hydro

hydro

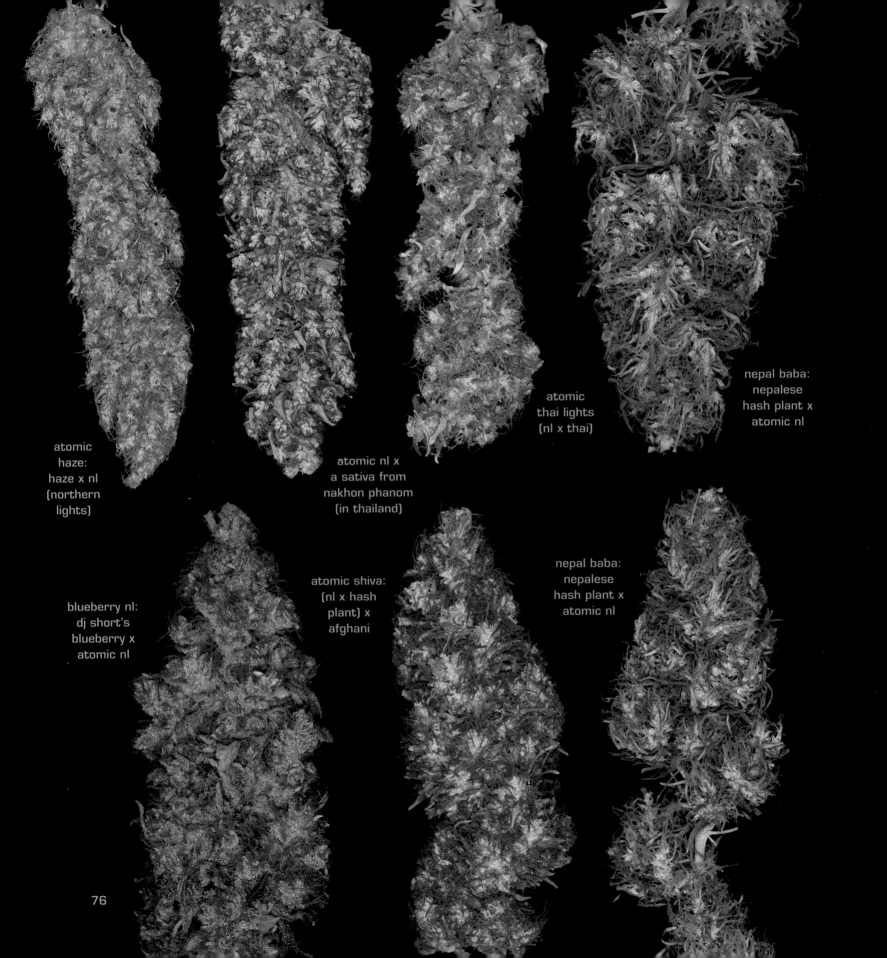

atomic
haze:
haze x nl
(northern
lights)

atomic nl x
a sativa from
nakhon phanom
(in thailand)

atomic
thai lights
(nl x thai)

nepal baba:
nepalese
hash plant x
atomic nl

blueberry nl:
dj short's
blueberry x
atomic nl

atomic shiva:
(nl x hash
plant) x
afghani

nepal baba:
nepalese
hash plant x
atomic nl

76

<< Dr. Atomic Strains

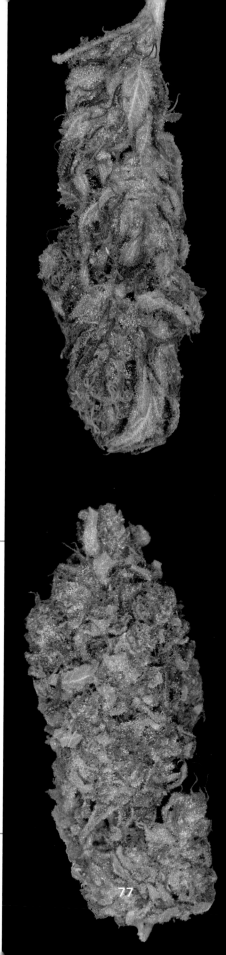

While visiting Vancouver, B.C., during the harvest of 2004, I was lucky enough to run into Dr. Atomic. The Doc has traveled extensively in Southeast Asia, the Himalayas, and the Middle East, collecting seeds along the way. He has bred these with top Dutch strains, creating a collection of lovely hybrids. The seeds are very reasonably priced, at least compared to some other seed companies. And I must say, I really enjoyed all the samples! At first I was a little turned off by the redness of the buds, but I was pleasantly surprised at the lush and diverse flavors present in each sample. I especially liked the Thai Lights and the Nepal Baba.

Dumpster >>

As the story goes, some head in Ohio is walking past a garbage dumpster, minding his own business, and notices a small ganja plant growing out of it. Perplexed, yet not one to turn down a gift from the Goddess, he snatches it up and brings it home. (One man gathers what another man spills.) As it turns out, the strain is incredible and unique! Nothing is known of her heritage, but to me she seems to be mostly an indica. She is commonly found in the Midwest, but thanks to the proliferating clone trade, Dumpster is becoming more available to the rest of us. The aroma is intense and skunky, with a tinge of something indescribable. This intense scent transitions to taste beautifully, leaving a thick, skunky taste on the palate. The high is very strong, definitely indica based, and quite long-lived as well. Also pictured (bottom right) is Dumpster x Mr Nice (see *Cannabible 2*, page 17), which was indeed nice but not as tasty as the pure Dumpster. (Note: There are now fake, wannabe Dumpster strains going around, known to many as "chumpster"!)

Early Girl is an old Sensi Seeds strain with a mostly indica background. The plants are generally tall and lanky for an indica, though occasional short and squat plants come up. The plants shown here were grown in Fort Bragg, California, where they did not fare well. Fort Brag is a coastal town, and the plants were infested with botrytis, powdery mildew, and a host of other problems. They were not quite what I would call "early" either, still in the ground in October. I would bet that Early Girl would be a much better plant in other parts of the world. The flavor is light and hashy, probably the weakest in the Sensi line.

Early Girl

Early Queen

I've always been impressed with Shantibaba's breeding skills, and Early Queen raises the bar. Early Queen, available from Mr Nice Seeds, is a very early strain indeed, finishing indoors in as little as six weeks. The Sea of Green method is the best way to grow her indoors, reportedly. Outdoors she usually reaches maturity by September, making her ideal for growers at higher latitudes. Early Queen is a three-way cross of Early Girl, Early Pearl, and Skunk. The sample pictured here was grown indoors organically in soil and produced thick, heady smoke with a lovely and complex aroma, hitting tangy and rich flavors ranging from earthen to rotten fruit—in a good way, if you can imagine that! The high was very enjoyable, quite giggly and euphoric. I found myself staring at the wall on more than one occasion. Outdoors, the plants will finish between late September and late October, depending on which phenotype is chosen. Early Queen is extremely resistant to various molds and does great in a light-deprivation setup.

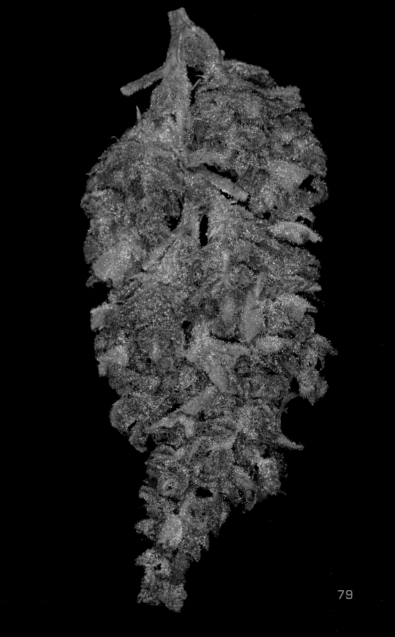

LIGHT DEP

There is a growing technique known as "light dep" or "light deprivation," which I will now shed some light on, pardon the pun. Cannabis plants flower when the days get shorter, which is why indoor growers provide a light cycle of twelve hours on, twelve hours off to induce flowering. This approximates the natural daily cycle of the sun. Though more involved, it's also possible to manipulate the lighting cycle with outdoor plants. That's what is known as the light-dep technique. Basically, some sort of structure is built around the plants, and every day and night at an exact time, the plants are covered or uncovered, keeping the light and dark periods at equal lengths. Most light-dep growers use a simple manual system, such as a PVC hoop structure, as shown below, and a large tarp or series of tarps that are pulled over the plants to provide darkness.

It's very important that all light is blocked during the dark periods, as even a tiny amount of light pollution can cause numerous problems, including hermaphrodites. It should be noted that certain strains are able to handle a little light pollution better than others. Light depping is a big commitment for the grower, as someone must be there at exactly the right times every day to change the covering, but the benefits are numerous. Most importantly, the crop is finished in June or July instead of October or November, which gets the plants out of the ground before the helicopters and thieves are usually looking. Many growers do a light-dep crop as well as a long-season crop, often doubling their yearly yields. Automated systems are available, but they are quite expensive.

Elvis >>

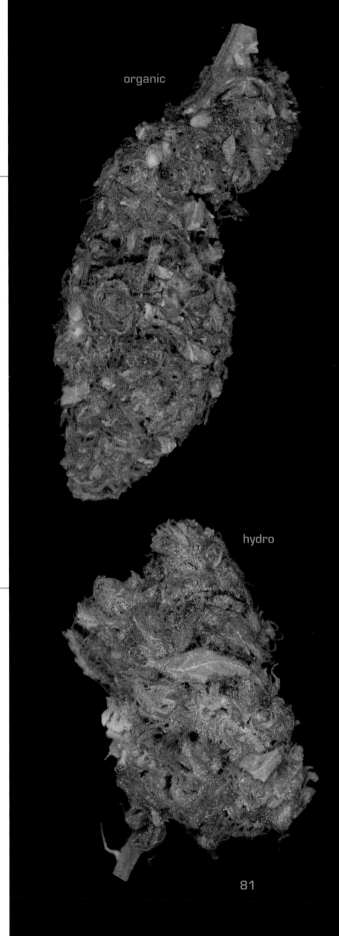

organic

hydro

Elvis is an elite clone mostly found on the East Coast. The King is in fact alive and kickin'. There are reportedly Elvis impersonators on the West Coast, but any true Elvis fan can easily identify the fakes. Elvis has such a bizarre and unique flavor that the only way to describe it is, you guessed it, polyester (hence the name). There are other flavors in there as well, resembling fresh berries and good-old dirt, but that trippy polyester flavor is what keeps you coming back. Elvis is a wonderful sativa, noted for its no-ceiling characteristic, meaning that the more you smoke, the higher you get—forever! I really like the high of Elvis; it's very uplifting and energetic, even creative. In the end, like its namesake, Elvis is quite chunky. Considering the sativa-based genetics, it's an extremely fast plant as well, finishing indoors in as little as fifty days. I recommend letting it go for sixty; it's worth the wait! Pictured are two different batches of indoor-grown Elvis, one organic and one hydro. The organic nug tasted at least ten times better, with many indescribably weird and yummy flavors revealing themselves that were not apparent with the hydroponically grown sample. Many growers of Elvis have reported the same thing.

Yet another Dutch Skunk selection, this one comes from Dutch Passion Seed Company. Created in 1996, Euforia is a viable commercial strain if your customers aren't too picky about flavor. It's not that the flavor is bad, it's just kind of weak and generic. Indoors, the plants mature in anywhere from forty-five to sixty days, depending on the phenotype selected. The yield is above average on this one, guaranteeing her a place in many Dutch commercial gardens. The high is average and unremarkable. This is probably my least favorite Dutch Passion strain.

Euforia

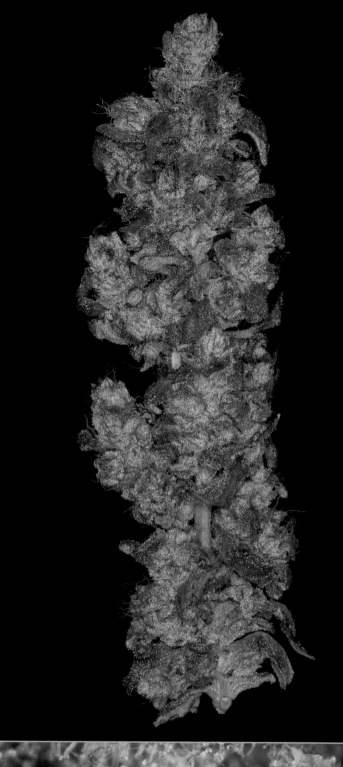

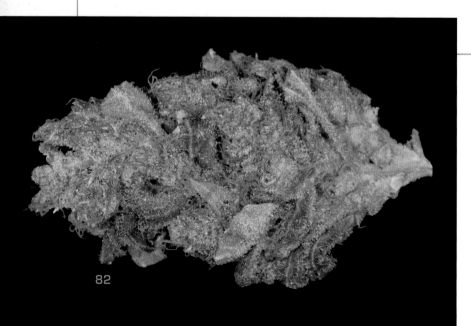

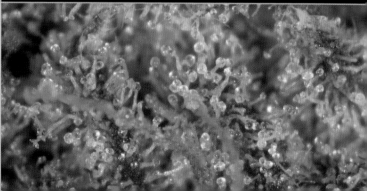

<< F-13

F-13 is a classic example of why DJ Short is my favorite breeder on the planet. Not only is this stunning and unique mostly sativa strain indescribably beautiful, the flavor and high are out of this world, too. F-13 is a heady sativa that would please even the pickiest connoisseur. The bud tastes, for lack of a more accurate description, like a Grateful Dead show. It's a wondrous and memorable combination of sage, Nag Champa, dank bud, hippie funk, cedar, and other exotic spices. The aftertaste is classic DJ Short blueness, with a hint of creamy vanilla—absolutely delicious. Brings me right back to the show. But the high is what really sets F-13 apart. It's snappy and clear, conversational and cerebral—exactly what I want in my jar! Considering the sativa-based lineage of F-13, she is quite fast, finishing indoors in as little as seven weeks. The yield is about average, which is actually great considering how low the yield is on most strains of this quality (Bubba Kush, OG Kush, Purps, Pure Kush, and so on).

organic indoor soil

organic indoor hydro

83

First Lady

Named for her fast flowering time, **First Lady** is a relatively new Sensi Seeds release that is a blend of indicas from Afghanistan and Pakistan. When grown indoors, this lady harvests in as little as forty days, making her a potentially valuable commercial strain or breeder. This is a typical indica, a stocky plant with thick and dark green leaves, short inter-nodal lengths, and a sleepy, narcotic high. Grown indoors hydroponically.

Funky Bitch and Golden Goat >>

Here we have easily the best herbs I've ever found anywhere between the East Coast and the West Coast. Believe it or not, these awesome buds were grown in the Midwest, where the laws are so harsh that I won't even mention what state they were grown in. **Funky Bitch** is a very special Hawaiian sativa x Romulan x Island Sweet Skunk phenotype that leans heavily toward the Hawaiian side of the spectrum, evident by the intense tropical and fruity flavors and the warped psychedelic high produced. This ganja really reminded me of good Hawaiian, an impressive feat to pull off indoors.

Even more impressive is the **Golden Goat,** another phenotype of the same heritage, this one leaning more toward the Sweet Skunk and Romulan genetics. **Golden Goat** has such an incredible smell—a complex blend of luscious fruits, vitamins, and a spicy haze note. To be honest, it reminded me of well-grown Trainwreck. The high from **Golden Goat** is extremely strong, a euphoric, heart-pounding, eye-reddening buzz than can be felt from head to toe, inducing heavy bouts of laughter and the munchies. My compliments to the grower of these fine herbs.

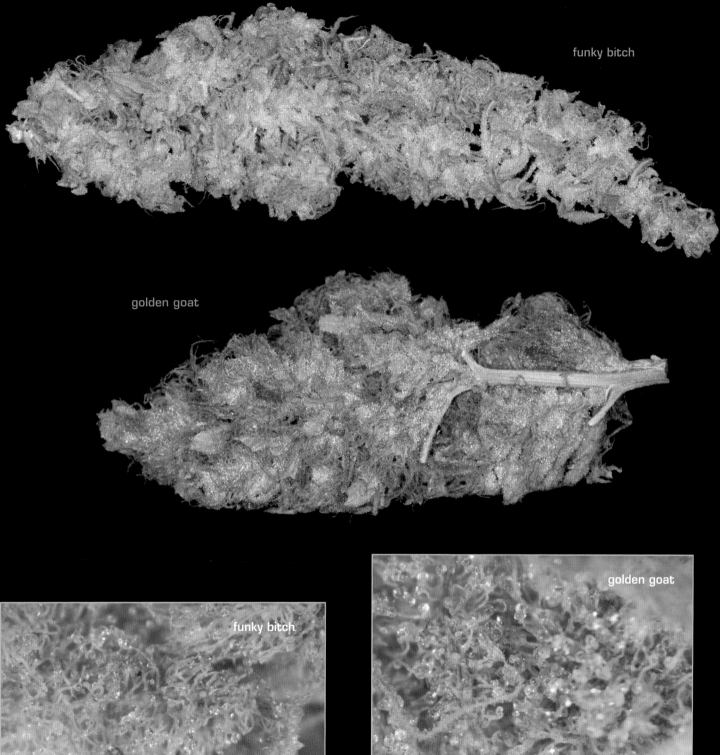

funky bitch

golden goat

golden goat

funky bitch

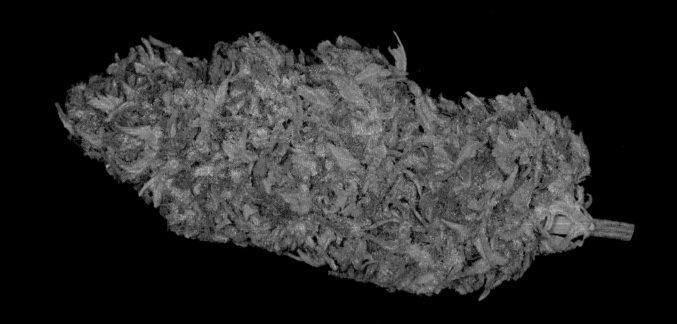

(G-13 x Blue Widow) x Killer Queen

To make this hybrid, NCGA crossed their Airborne G-13 (page 22) x Blue Widow (see *Cannabible 2*, page 32) with Killer Queen, a British Columbia Growers Association (BCGA) cross of G-13 (see *Cannabible 1*, page 73) and Cindy 99 (see *Cannabible 2*, page 36). NCGA's G-13 x Blue Widow, known to produce dense flowers even in partial shade, is a great strain for growing under trees. Interestingly, it's not cut out for full sun, at least in Northern California, where it gets intensely hot during the summer months. When crossed with Killer Queen, the result was a plant that loves full sun, and this cross can easily yield over five pounds per plant if given enough sunlight, food, and water. Unfortunately, with Killer Queen came a susceptibility to botrytis, aka bud rot. The flavor of this herb is skunky and fruity while also possessing a slight acridity. Grown outdoors in Mendocino, California.

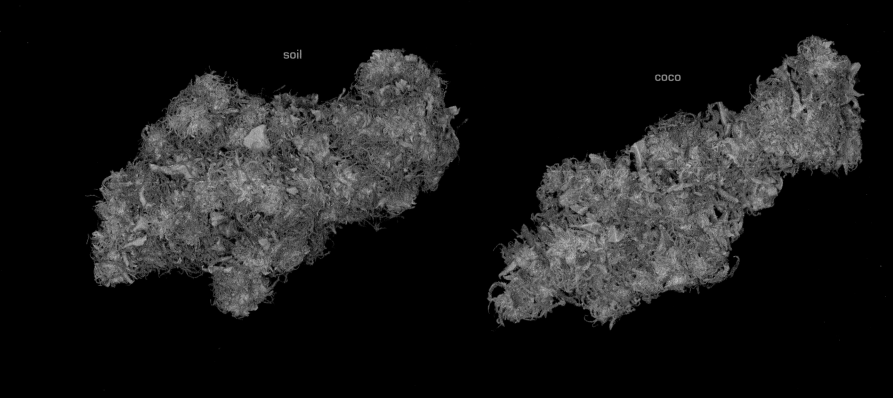

soil

coco

grown in
coco

88

<< Garlic Bud

This old-school Sensi Seeds Afghani strain was one of the first kind buds I ever scored. It's nice to see that it's still around. Though it's been almost two decades since I scored those Garlic nugs, I remember them very well. They really reeked of garlic in a sort of good way, and it was strong smoke, too. As far as this Garlic Bud is concerned, neither the grower nor myself was impressed with the strain when grown indoors. The yield was good and the flowering time acceptably fast, but the flavors were lacking, and the high was mild at best. Pictured are two different indoor-grown batches. One was grown in soil, the other in coco growing medium. I've heard that the strain still kicks ass when grown outdoors, so there is still hope.

Ginger Ale >>

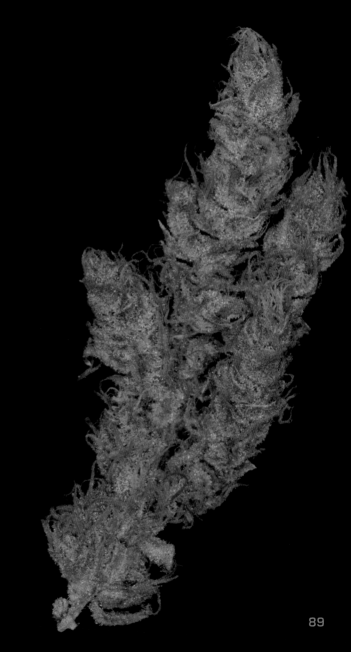

On a trip to Amsterdam, Mr. Soul, a breeder from Brothers Grimm seed company, purchased a bud of Jack Herer in which he found some seeds. Though the father of these seeds is unknown, they produced some exquisite herb, and three female "keepers" were found. They were named Princess, Genius (*Cannabible 2*, page 67), and Cafe Girl. Crosses from these girls compromise most of the Brothers Grimm lineup. The Cafe Girl was crossed with Cinderella 88, another Brothers Grimm project in which multiple backcrosses were being made to the original Princess clone (a process known as "cubing"), and thus was created Ginger Ale. The bud does in fact taste like ginger ale, though I know the flavor of the bud I sampled would have been much stronger and better had it been grown organically. Seven weeks of flowering is usually more than enough for Ginger Ale to finish. The yield is above average, the high warm and mellow.

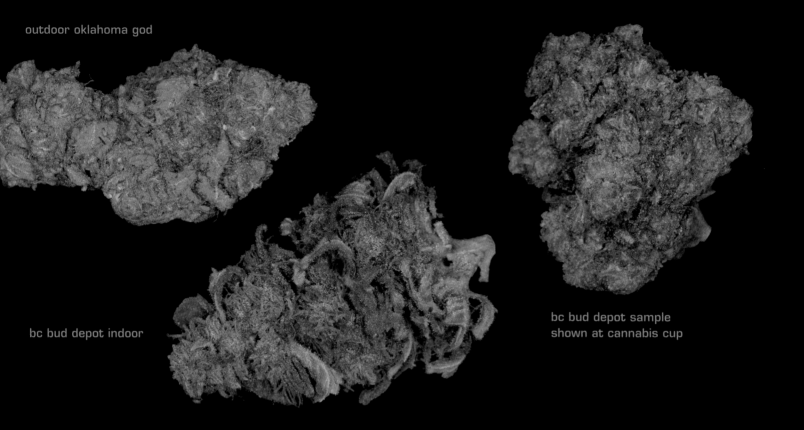

outdoor oklahoma god

bc bud depot indoor

bc bud depot sample
shown at cannabis cup

Pretty presumptuous to name a strain God, wouldn't you say? It must be pretty amazing herb, right? However, I sampled three different versions and none of them greatly impressed me. God is a clone that's been in Canada for many years. A company called Jordan of the Islands was the first to sell a version of it, and this is a pretty good strain. It has a lovely smell of dried apricots and a pleasant fruity flavor. I didn't exactly see God after smoking it, but it was nice medicine. Then there is the BC Bud Depot version, which somehow won the Cannabis Cup in 2004 despite it being mediocre herb at best (they must have kissed some serious *High Times* ass). I sampled the bud directly from the "winners" and, to be honest, felt no inspiration to even finish the joint. They claim to have crossed the original God clone with Hawaiian and Purple Indica. Sounds delicious; I wonder what happened! Nearly a year later I got another sample that was grown indoors in California, which also did nothing for me. It had a weak sort of fruity smell but tasted slightly bitter and unpleasant. There have been many negative reports about BC Bud Depot on the Web. I would suggest finding God elsewhere. (LSD or yoga, perhaps?)

God

TISSUE CULTURE

BY CHIMERA

Many growers are perpetually on the hunt for the holy grail of cannabis, and it seems that new must-have varieties come to the forefront every year. Just looking through any of the Cannabibles gets many gardeners' juices flowing, with dreams of one particular plant growing in their own garden. However, when these gardeners try to obtain some of these strains, they run into a problem: Many of these selections are "clone only"—no seeds accurately representing the individual clone are available.

Even when seeds are available, cultivators often find that very few, if any, of the grown plants match the advertised description of the variety—even when the seeds come directly from the original clone specimen. The reason is simple: Just as none of you readers are identical to your mother or father, no cannabis seed is identical to its mother or father.

In the legal horticulture industry, when a breeder or grower finds a unique and desirable specimen to cultivate, it can be legally multiplied and distributed as cuttings. Growers all over the world can purchase or trade these clones so they may each enjoy the unique qualities the individual has to offer.

Due to the illicit nature of cannabis, however, clones are not sold openly, and although clones are traded within circles of growers, most growers must primarily rely on growing from seed and looking for special gems themselves. This is often an inconvenience, as many seed selections sold are extremely variable and yield a high percentage of less-than-desirable individuals. This often means growing out many batches of seed to find highly desirable plants to use as mothers for future cultivation, at great expense in both wasted space and seed costs. Crops grown for selection from seed are less uniform, yield less, and produce a varied quality of product.

Imagine if growers were able to buy preselected, highly desirable clones that grew to the exact specifications of the description and produced a known-quality final product. In fact, this is possible via a technology known as "tissue culture."

Tissue culture is the art of growing plant parts in a sterile medium that offers all the nutrients necessary for growth. In many cases, shoot tips are grown in a gel-like medium, and the plants actually grow without roots; sometimes they even grow without light. Sunlight is usually required for plant growth because it powers photosynthesis, which in turn creates the sugars needed for the plant to sustain life. Because glucose is often added to the growth medium in tissue culture, the plants can use it as a carbon source and thus grow without light.

There are various forms of tissue culture, from growing single cells into undifferentiated callus (akin to plant stem cells) to micropropagation of shoot tips. Undifferentiated cells can be fooled into believing they're destined to become embryos, and their growth can be directed via hormones to produce somatic embryos—embryo-like structures that are derived from established cell lines, not via sexual reproduction. Micropropagation occurs when tiny cuttings are grown in an agar medium in petri dishes, glass jars, or test tubes. Both somatic embryos and microcuttings are genetic clones of the donor tissue and are easily shipped discreetly in the mail. Once grown, the end result of either method is a plant identical in every way to the plant that donated its cells to the culture.

In the course of my research, I learned of a technology that had never been applied to cannabis—the concept of artificial seeds. I discussed the idea with various industry folks in both Holland and Canada, and none had ever heard of the technology, let alone tried to apply it to cannabis. Artificial seeds are plant embryos or tiny growth shoot tips that have been encapsulated in small protective beadlike objects. They look like small marbles or large jellylike fish eggs and can be stored for relatively long periods of time (about a year) and shipped as seeds are today. They do require a certain degree of care to propagate, and they're not as easy to cultivate as typical seeds. However, they allow cannabis breeders and growers to share highly desirable clones on a global basis. Just consider the possibility of being able to obtain an exact clone of every strain pictured and described in this book.

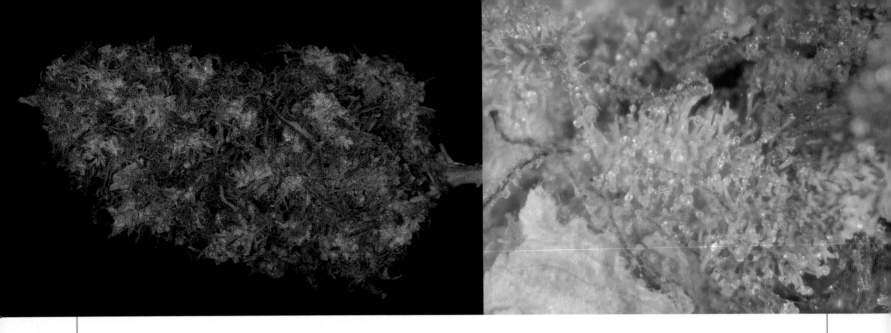

An Australian breeder who goes by the name Wallyduck made this supertasty hybrid by crossing a very pine-apple-tasting phenotype of Cindy 99 (see *Cannabible 2*, page 36) with Golden Skush, which is a cross of Hindu Kush (see *Cannabible 1*, page 89) and Skunk #1 (see *Cannabible 1*, page 161). This herb really does taste like a golden pineapple. (For a real treat, smoke some while eating pineapple.) There is a luscious sweetness that's almost soapy, as well as a strong suggestion of mangoes and other tropical and fruity flavors to delight the palate. The high from Golden Pineapple is very smooth and enjoyable—a nice blend of trippy head high and euphoric body buzz. Expertly grown indoors using an organic hydro setup.

Golden Pineapple

Not to be mistaken with butane hash extract that is also called Goo sometimes, the strain Goo is a clone sometimes seen around Oaksterdam, the heavily cannabis-infused section of downtown Oakland. This mostly indica strain is reportedly a cross of Hindu Kush (see *Cannabible 1*, page 89) and Bubbleberry. Though these samples were expertly and organically grown in the great outdoors of Lakeport, California, I was not very impressed with the strain (at least when grown outdoors). The plants were very colorful and beautiful to look at, but the aroma and flavor had a generic and simple sweetness, with soft woody undertones. I was bored after one hit. The high was murky and lethargic, even sleepy. I suspect that this is one of those rare strains that does much better indoors, at least as far as flavor is concerned.

Goo >>

<< Granddaddy Purple

Ever since Purple Urkel became all the rage on the West Coast connoisseur herb scene, demand for the product has been overwhelming and insatiable. The Urkel is tricky to grow, isn't a large yielder, and isn't particularly early. The need arose for a fatter and quicker version of Urkel. By crossing it with a Big Bud male from Sensi Seeds stock, growers have basically achieved this goal. Granddaddy Purple (GDP) is relatively new to the scene but already has a great reputation. These plants were grown outdoors organically in Northern California and had not turned purple (yet). This one depends on colder temperatures to turn purple. GDP is a great strain, and I certainly see why so many people like it, but personally I prefer the pure Purple Urkel. It has a more exotic flavor and a better high as well. But please don't get me wrong—I would happily puff on some GDP any day! The flavor is sweet and perfumey, with a pungent bottom end, but as I said, not quite as exotic as the pure Urkel. The high is strong and felt mostly in the body.

DOES POT CAUSE CANCER?

For the longest time I have wondered about one particular facet of cannabis science. If pot smoke contains four times as much tar as tobacco smoke, as well as many of the other carcinogens found in cigarette smoke, as they say, why do we never hear of people who smoke only cannabis getting cancer? Science is finally providing some answers.

It started in 1974, in a little-known study in which researchers at the Medical College of Virginia, funded by the National Institutes of Health, set out to find evidence that marijuana damages the immune system. Instead, they found that THC slowed the growth of three kinds of cancer. (The DEA quickly shut down the Virginia study and all further research into the relationship between cannabis and tumors.) Several major population studies have shown no link between marijuana smoking and a higher risk of lung cancer, but we all know people who've gotten cancer from smoking cigarettes. In fact, a Jamaican study showed that regular users of marijuana not only had a lower risk of cancer than nonusers, they also had a slightly higher IQ and a longer life span!

Consider this: All American cigarettes contain significant levels of polonium 210, which produces the same kind of radiation given off by the plutonium in atom bombs. The tobacco plant's roots and leaves are just super at absorbing radioactive elements from chemical phosphate fertilizers that are required by U.S. law, as well as from naturally occurring radiation in the soil, water, and air. According to C. Everett Koop, this radioactivity—not tar—accounts for at least 90 percent of all smoking-related lung cancer. Tobacco kills over 400,000 people in the United States alone every year, not to mention polluting the world for those of us who still like to breathe clean air.

Although cigarette and marijuana smoke both contain large amounts of cancer-causing chemicals, there are other special qualities in marijuana that prevent it from promoting lung cancer, according to recent studies. The difference lies in the opposing actions of THC in marijuana versus nicotine in tobacco. To put it simply, nicotine has several effects that promote various cancers, but THC acts in ways that counter the cancer-causing chemicals in marijuana smoke. To put it another way, THC actually reduces the carcinogenic potential of the smoke. As an example, recent lab research indicates that nicotine, the active and highly addictive ingredient in tobacco, activates an enzyme that converts certain chemicals in tobacco smoke into a cancer-promoting form. THC, on the other hand, inhibits the enzyme necessary to activate the carcinogens found in ganja smoke.

Another major difference between ganja and tobacco is in the effects on the immune system. Smoke from either sends irritants into the respiratory system that trigger an inflammatory response, which includes the generation of cell-damaging substances called "free radicals." These particles are believed to contribute to a wide range of diseases, including cancer. But cannabinoids—those found in marijuana *and* the versions found naturally in the body—have been shown to decrease this inflammatory response. Another difference between the effects of smoking cannabis versus tobacco has to do with cells that line the respiratory tract. These cells have receptors that act as docks for nicotine, but there are no similar receptors for THC and other cannabinoids. These cells often progress into tumors when nicotine docks to them. THC, on the other hand, doesn't act this way in the respiratory tract. In fact, recent research shows that in the brain, where for some not-so-strange reason there are built-in cannabinoid receptors, THC can even protect cells and keep them from dying after being damaged from an injury or stroke.

Furthermore, compounds found in cannabis have been shown to kill numerous types of cancer, including leukemia and lymphoma, glioma (the cause of some brain tumors), pheochromocytoma, and cancers of the lung, breast, prostate, and skin. Think about it: Science has proven that THC and other cannabis extracts—benign substances occurring in nature—destroy brain tumors. You'd think it would be front-page news in every newspaper and medical journal in the world!

So to answer my question Does pot cause cancer? No. And not only does it not cause cancer, it can cure it, too!

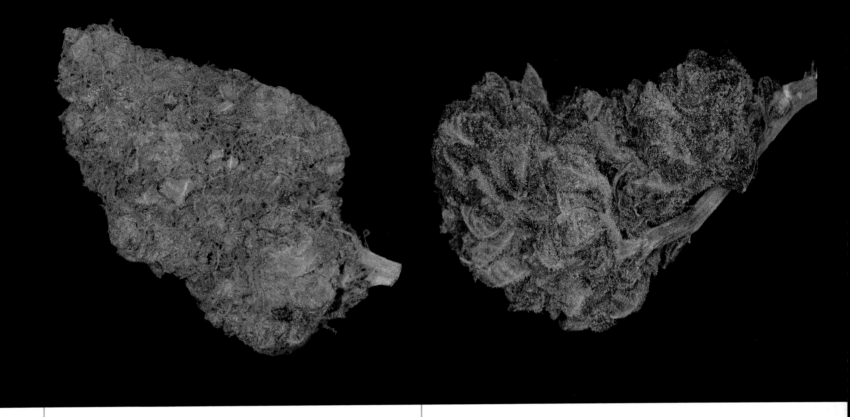

Grape Ape is a strain that is mostly available in clone form from some of the cannabis buyers clubs in the East Bay area. I've heard that the strain still exists in seed form as well, but clones are making their way around much more efficiently. Grape Ape has a delicious grapy flavor with other luscious fruity tones as well. This one's scent consists almost entirely of high notes, with one particularly earthy and ineffable bottom tone. Grape Ape is mostly an indica and has the strong narcotic high that many medicinal users seem to prefer. Some medical users have reported an antianxiety characteristic to this strain. Samples from two different growers are shown. They don't even look related. Go figure.

Grape Ape

Another stellar new release from DJ Short, Grape Krush seems to have no weaknesses whatsoever. The aroma, an intensely luscious grape candy explosion that truly makes the mouth water, is outstanding. This seductive scent transitions to flavor beautifully, especially in a vaporizer. The high is top-notch, a perfect blend of body-relaxing buzz and heady mental stimulation. The yields from Grape Krush are very high, sometimes downright astonishing. Two pounds per 1,000-watt light have been reported. Finally, the flowering time, at around seven to eight weeks, is very respectable for herb of this quality. Interestingly, the strain often exhibits strange leaf deformities, usually the crinkle type. Luckily, this does not seem to affect the yield or finished product at all. Kudos to DJ Short for releasing such awesome and unique strains. Pictured are batches by two different growers, one from California and one from BC. They were nearly identical, showing the stability of this strain.

Grape Krush >>

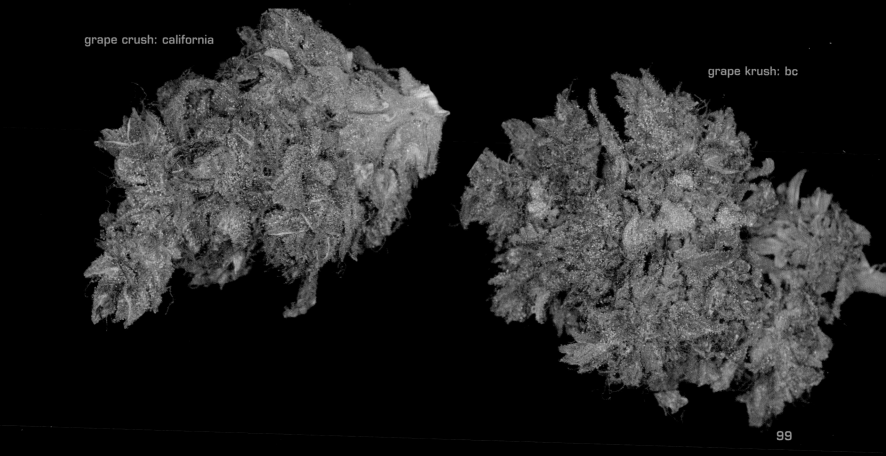

grape crush: california

grape krush: bc

Grape Mist

Another of the Northern California Mist hybrids, Grape Mist balances out at 50:50 indica to sativa. She stays short and compact during flowering and produces solid flowers that smell as sweet as freshly smashed fruit—mostly grapes. This aroma transitions to flavor beautifully, and a good vaporizer really reveals the flavor. Expertly and consciously grown indoors organically in soil.

100

Great Garberville

This old-school inbred line from Garberville, California, was originally created by crossing a Thai strain with an old Afghani-Hawaiian hybrid. After many years of inbreeding, the strain now breeds true. There are two main phenotypes found within Great Garberville: a purple one and a green one. Both have lovely aromas and flavors, the purple leaning slightly toward grapes, while the green has more of an earthy/hashy flavor. The yield is quite high, and outdoors she's capable of producing multipound plants. As for the high, this is potent herb, with a thoroughly narcotic body to it. These samples were grown from Reeferman seed stock outdoors on Vancouver Island.

Green Giant

Spice Brothers Seeds have released this commercial strain, an indica-dominant cross of Big Bud (see *Cannabible 1*, page 35) and Shiva Skunk (see *Cannabible 1*, page 157). This girl really packs on the weight, but watch out for the stink; without good carbon filters, your whole block may reek of skunk. Indoors, Green Giant can be harvested anywhere between fifty and seventy days, while outdoors she finishes in the middle of October. The flavor of Green Giant is your typical skunky indica, nothing overwhelming, but decent. The high is also typical indica, narcotic but manageable for half an hour or so. After that I just took a nap. These samples were grown outdoors in Mendocino, California.

G-Sus

I know, these names are getting hilarious, maybe even borderline blasphemous. But the Creator must have a sense of humor and did in fact create cannabis, so I think we're okay. According to Reeferman, you have to go through G-Sus to reach God. G-Sus, predictably, is a cross of Airborne G-13 (see page 22) and God (page 90). A cutting from the Jordan of the Islands God was used, and crossing it with Airborne G-13 produced an indica-dominant hybrid of couchlocking proportions. The strain is easy to grow, producing dense and oily nuggets with a smell that almost reminded me of Elvis, but not quite. The plants finish in eight to nine weeks indoors, while outdoors they'll finish in mid-October. Now wait, if Reeferman created G-Sus, wouldn't that make him . . . ?

HAWAII

puna budda

To this day, the Big Island of Hawaii produces some of the kindest herb ever grown. There are countless strains floating around, ranging from psychedelic old Hawaiian sativas to the latest Dutch offerings. It is especially difficult to grow in Hawaii, and between the incessant helicopter patrols (Operation Green Harvest), thieves, animals, rain, insects, mold, and every other imaginable threat, it's amazing that anyone still does it. Add to this the fact that the average plant grown outdoors in Hawaii produces only seven to fourteen grams (due mostly to the short tropical growing seasons), and the often-exorbitant prices and lack of exports start to make sense. You don't get much of da kine. So the mainland doesn't see much Hawaiian, but if you can get it the quality is unbeatable.

Herb grown in Hawaii, like that grown in other tropical locales, often tastes very tropical and packs a high that's almost like tripping. Some believe that plants grown in the tropics produce more THC as protection from the sun's intense UV rays at those latitudes. Often due to the extremely wet conditions that prevail in Hawaii, the herb can't be dried perfectly, let alone cured properly, and it definitely suffers as a result. But something about Hawaiian herb is so completely amazing that it still manages to rank with the world's best. All of these samples were grown outdoors organically on the Big Island of Hawaii.

blueberry

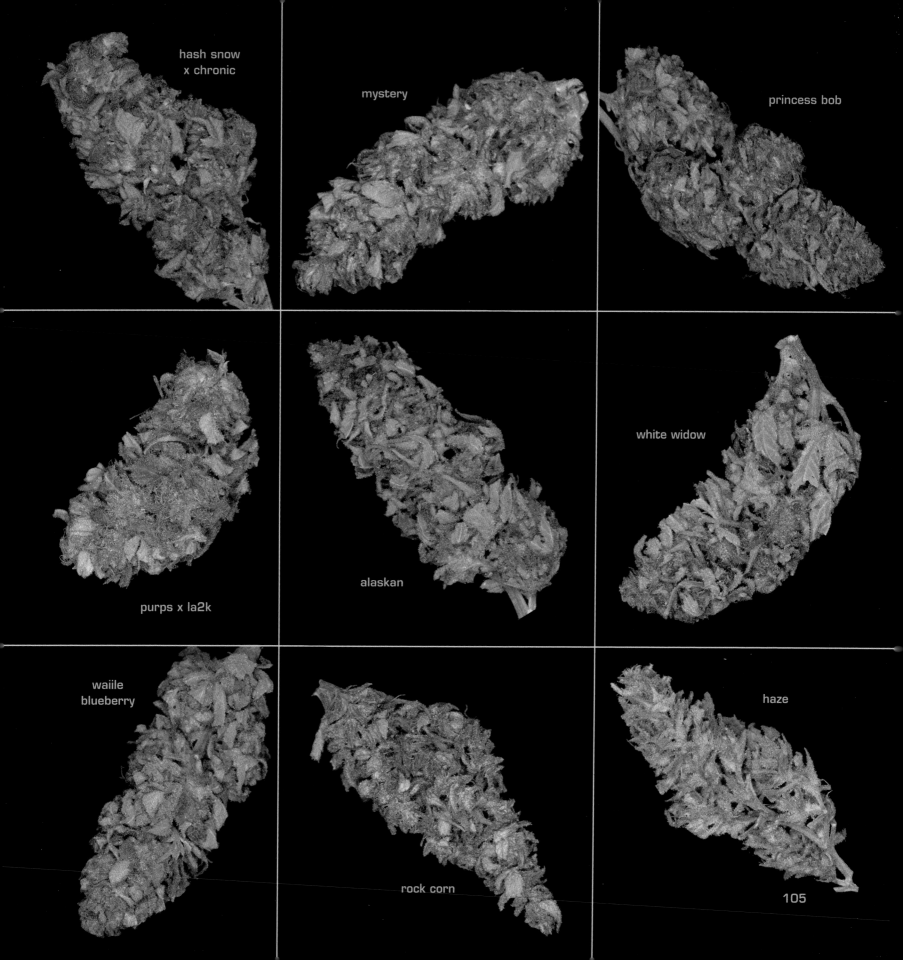

hash snow
x chronic

mystery

princess bob

purps x la2k

alaskan

white widow

waiile
blueberry

rock corn

haze

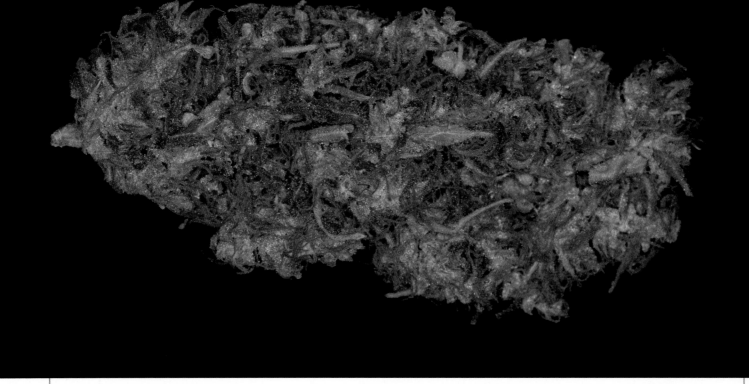

According to Arjan, the breeder of this 2003 Cannabis Cup–winning strain from Green House Seed Company, **Hawaiian Snow** is a cross of a Hawaiian strain from the Puna district and a "Haze from Laos." I don't know exactly what Haze Arjan is talking about, as Laos genetics are not a part of true Haze, and I doubt there are people growing true Haze in Laos from which he could have acquired seeds. But whatever it is, I will say that it's exotic and delicious herb. According to Arjan, **Hawaiian Snow** has been tested at 23.7 percent THC. I would love to see that test. I did enjoy the **Hawaiian Snow**. I was heavily medicated after half a fatty, even with my ridiculously high tolerance while in Amsterdam. The samples that won the cup were the first organically grown samples ever entered by Green House—a big part of why it won, in my opinion. This ganja had a beautiful and rich flavor with tones ranging from spicy candy to earthen dankness. The flowering time is said to be twelve to thirteen weeks indoors, longer than the average by today's indica-based standards but well worth the wait according to this sativa lover.

Hawaiian Snow

The Original Haze

Flying Dutchmen Seeds in Holland has been working with this strain for twenty years. They've kept this version pure, so this is valuable breeding material, folks. Haze has an awesome cerebral high that's somewhat racy at times. In pure form, these babies want to go one hundred days or more indoors, but outdoors is where they really prefer to be, in my opinion, assuming the climate permits. Expect harvest to come in December or possibly even later outdoors. The flavor of this killer sativa is spicy, sweet, and sour all at once, with an extremely spicy exhalation. This sample was grown indoors organically in soil. Not recommended for commercial growers, due to the huge size and lengthy flowering time.

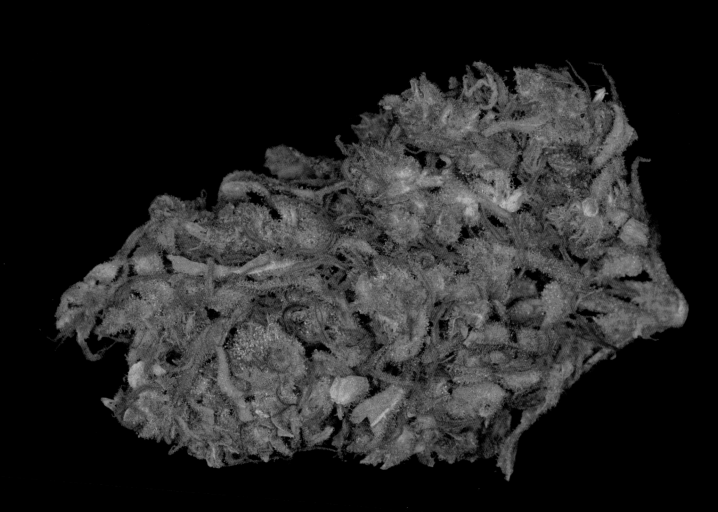

Heavy Duty Fruity

This release from T.H.Seeds in Amsterdam should be very appealing to any commercial grower, as it's one of the heaviest-yielding strains out there, hence the name. The strain was made by crossing a Killin Garberville male with a Mendocino Hash Plant x Seattle Big Bud female. Once again, West Coast genetics leading the way! Heavy Duty Fruity (HDF) has a fruity and sweet flavor with a touch of spice if you find the right phenotype. The strain is not known for being particularly stable, but a pack of seeds should definitely turn up some keepers. The high from HDF really depends on the phenotype chosen, but in my experience it's a cerebral and potent herb. The best phenotypes usually finish in about eight weeks—impressive for a strain with more of a sativa high. Grown, photographed, and smoked outdoors in Mendocino, California.

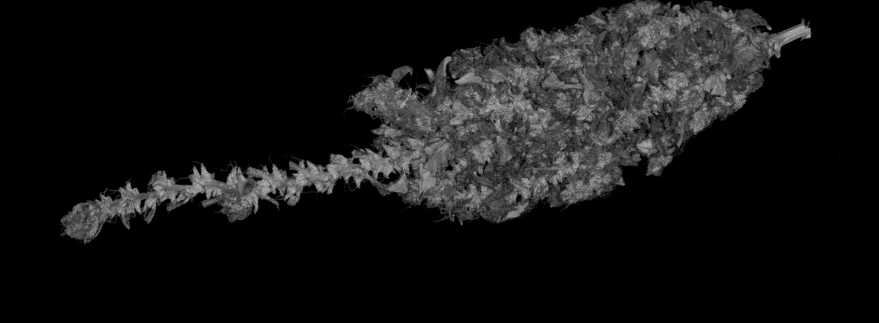

The good people at Legends Seeds took a legendary
strain indeed, Rene (page 185), and crossed her with
a Blueberry male from DJ Short's latest projects. The
resultant hybrid is wicked good and unique as well.
The samples I got definitely leaned toward the Blueberry papa, evident by the strong blue flavor as well as
the classic Thai spindly bract structure shooting from
the tips of buds. (Blueberry comes from mostly Thai
genetics.) This herb has a lush and complex flavor, with
funky, fruity, spicy, citrusy, and notably earthy tones
dancing about my olfactory senses. This girl tastes
even better than she smells, and strangely, despite this
sample being grown in a hydroponic setup, the taste is
really earthy. (I almost never taste earthy tones, which
I adore, in hydroponically grown herb.) The nutrients
used in this setup were all organic, which greatly
helped matters. The high from Highend is very strong
and heady, yet not in any way debilitating. My compliments to the grower of this fine herb.

Highend

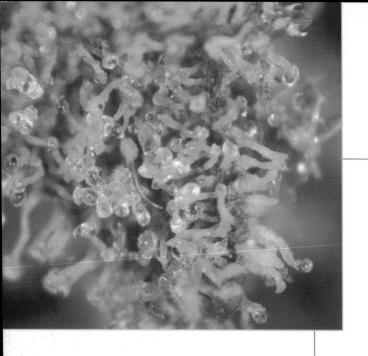

The Hog

Hogsbreath (see *Cannabible 1*, page 90) is a superstinky San Diego strain that's been around since the late 1980s. It is reportedly a cross of a very special Hindu Kush (see *Cannabible 1*, page 89) and Afghani (see *Cannabible 1*, page 27). Hogsbreath reeks like bad breath and garlic—but in a good way, like the bad breath of your sweetie, who just ate a clove of garlic and slept all night, with no toothbrushing. T.H.Seeds got the real deal and brought it to Amsterdam, where they crossed it with a male Mazar-i-Sharif from cultivators choice in '93, and released the line as **the Hog.** The key here is to select the phenotype that most resembles the Hogsbreath. You'll know it when you smell it. Think dirty feet (but in a good way). **The Hog** is a heavy yielder of greasy indica flowers that mature indoors in approximately fifty-five days. This one won the 2002 Cannabis Cup for best indica, and for good reason. Grown indoors organically in soil.

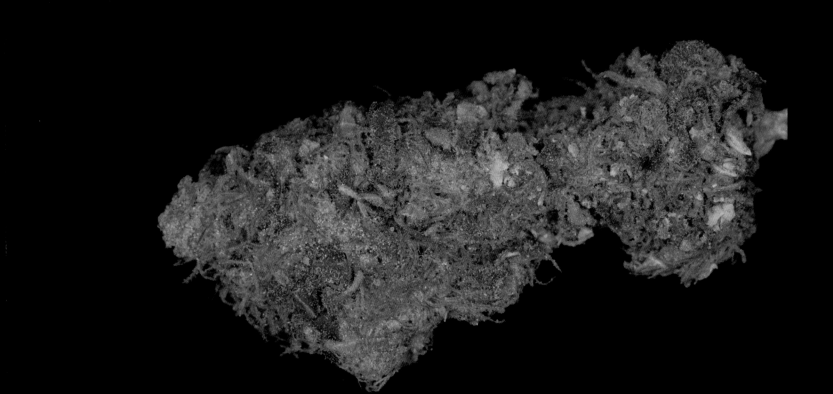

Jasmine, a strain I came across while nugget hunting in Humboldt, is a cross of a '96 Sensi Seeds Silver Haze and Golden Boy, a strain from Calgary. The sample I got was grown indoors organically in coco growing medium and had a delicate and beautiful aroma, definitely hinting of fine Jasmine tea but also with a suggestion of assorted sweet fruits and agave nectar. Deep in the background there is a lovely hazy spiciness that brings it all home. Luckily this fine aroma transitions to flavor completely, making for a very tasty and enjoyable fatty or vape hit. Jasmine is a great cloner, sometimes rooting in as little as five days. She likes a lot of food and a lot of light, and finishes indoors in 50–60 days. Outdoors, she finishes around October 31, and is fully capable of producing five pound plants if given enough food, light, and water. Compliments to the grower and breeder of this beaut. This commercial grower ditched his previous chemical nutrient formula and switched to Humboldt Flower Products OG A and OG B and Humboldt Hunney. In the end, the buds were bigger, the bracts more swollen, and the herb tasted much sweeter. The switch was very easy to make, and the results were profound. The products are made in Humboldt, California, and I highly recommend them.

Jasmine

indoor organic

outdoor organic

111

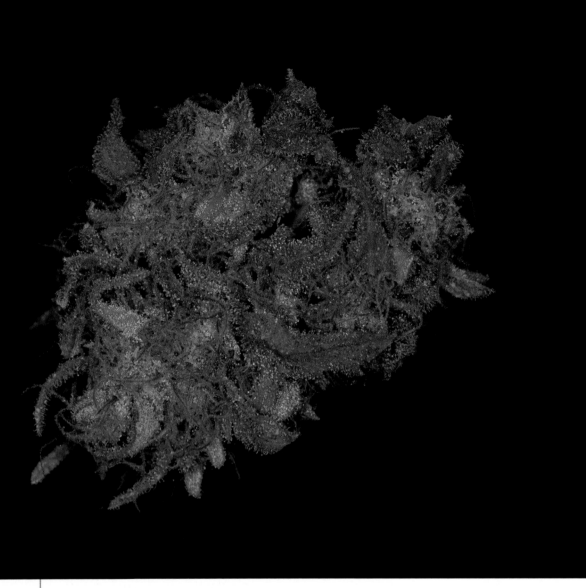

Jedi

Jedi is a clone-only strain from San Diego that's quite popular in Southern California. Two different stories about its lineage are circulating: one claims that it's a cross of White Rhino and Lions Gate, and the other says it's a Skywalker hybrid. If I had to guess, I'd say that it's White Rhino x Lions Gate. We may never know for sure; such is the nature of cannabis strains. **Jedi** is a dense indica-dominant plant with a trippy taste and smell that's difficult to describe. It's sweet and kind of balmy with a strange tangy nose. The high is above average in strength and felt mostly in the body. The plant grows with a large dominant cola and nice large side branches, producing a crop with no small buds or "larf." This sample was expertly grown outdoors organically in Northern California. Within minutes of smoking a bowl, my ability to use the force noticeably increased.

Juliet

Juliet is a breeding experiment by a highly skilled grower/breeder who goes by the name of John Lee Pedimore. A Cindy 99 female (see *Cannabible 2*, page 36) was pollinated by a "NYCD" male. (I use quotation marks because the NYCD used in this cross is the one sold by Soma Seeds in Amsterdam, which barely resembles the real Diesel, if at all.) At the same time, the same strains were crossed the other way ("NYCD" female x C99 male). The resultant strain, as you might have guessed, was named Romeo. Seeds from both crosses were given to several other growers for more testing. The goal was to see if one sex contributed more genes to a cross than the other. Interestingly, it would appear that in most cases, the mother plant brings more to the cross. I wonder if this applies to humans? Juliet has a very pleasant flavor that's a bit hard to put words on. It's more herbal than fruity, with a slight touch of spice and perhaps a bit of citrus. The high is very heady and positive. There is no burnout, which is always nice. Grown indoors organically in a hydroponic setup, by the man himself! Thanks JLP!

TOP TEN NECESSITIES FOR CANNABIS CONNOISSEURSHIP

1. **Connoisseur-grade organic herb.** Can't find it? Grow your own! This one can't be skipped.

2. **Clean glass bong.** Clean it often, as flavor is greatly enhanced by smoking through clean glass. Bubblers—small, handheld glass water pipes—work great, too. Use rubbing alcohol and salt to clean the glass. The salt won't dissolve and acts as an abrasive to knock off the accumulated resin.

3. **Club rolling papers.** These are the connoisseur's choice. They are unbleached and have no glue. (Who wants to smoke bleach or glue?) Rip off the edge of the paper and the rough fibers act like glue. Hemp papers taste like hemp, and all of the other rolling papers out there noticeably decrease the flavor of a joint, too. (I'm not a spokesman for Club, I promise!) A fantastic new option is transparent cigarette papers. They are made of 100 percent plant cellulose, have no flavor, and look really cool because they are clear.

4. **Vaporizer.** The technology is still in its infancy, but there are some great vaporizers out there. Vaporizers heat the herb just enough to release the active compounds without combustion and, thus, without any of the nasty things that come along with smoke. My favorites are the VRIP and the Valloon (www.vriptech.com), Hot Glass (www.freshheadies.com), and Super Vapezilla (www.wickedroots.com).

5. **Herb grinder.** The greatest stoner invention since the bong. They quickly grind the herb to perfect joint or vaporization consistency without losing half the resin on your fingers.

6. **Anything that eliminates the use of plastic lighters,** with their nasty butane fumes and toxic flint smoke. A device called Phedor is the connoisseur's choice (www.wickedroots.com). Untreated matches (burned past the sulfur), a magnifying glass for solar hits (see *Cannabible 1*, page 36), or a high-quality lighter with cleaner-burning fuel are some other good options. You will be astounded by how much better your ganja tastes when you eliminate the butane fumes and flint smoke. The high is also noticeably cleaner. I've found that the headaches I sometimes had after a long day of puffing herb have stopped since I eliminated lighters and butane from my life. Consider this: Smokers of top-quality cigars would never consider using a disposable butane lighter to light a cigar. Cigar aficionados tell me that if you light a top-notch cigar (*gross!*) with a Bic lighter, then put it out and relight it a month later, you would still notice the foul butane taste left behind from the original lighting. These connoisseurs use specialty wooden matches sold in cigar shops. There is something to be learned here from our carcinogenic cousins.

7. **Glass jars for herb storage.** Glass is truly the best way to store cannabis. Plastic bags and containers can impart a plastic flavor to the medicine. Glass ensures that the herb stays untainted and uncrushed. Many glassblowers are selling artistic custom nug jars, the perfect blend of beauty and function!

8. **Good music.** Life (and especially fine herb) is so much more enjoyable with good music. Plus, when extremely high, one often gets new

insights to the meaning of the music, which was undoubtedly created by someone who was very high.

9. **Munchies.** Let's face it: Smoking superkind ganja is going to give you some serious munchies, so it's best to have some clean and healthy options around. Natural food stores have organic and much-less-processed versions of all the things we crave, without all the chemicals and garbage found in most munchies. Think fruit!

10. **A sense of taste that hasn't been destroyed by smoking cigarettes.** This is a big one. When you smoke cigarettes, your sense of taste and smell, which are closely related, are greatly diminished, if not destroyed (not to mention that you offend any noncigarette smokers, who *can* still smell). How can you appreciate the brilliantly diverse flavors of fine cannabis with most of your olfactory senses destroyed? (Or even worse, if you're dead!) You cannot. Please quit immediately.

11. Oh yeah, and of course the **Cannabible series** in hardcover.

Kings Kross is Reeferman's spin on a highly coveted old-school Vancouver Island clone known as King (no relation). Kings Kross is a backcross to the King, which was blended with an old Kush strain, which became known as Charles Kush, which originally came from early Seed Bank Kush lines. So the lineage looks like this: (King x Charles Kush) x King. Undisturbed, the dried bud smells like a blend of dried kitchen herbs. When a bud is broken apart, the nose shifts to this outrageous and exotic trippy floral thing with hints of pomegranate, pine, and plum and other indescribable tones. Kings Kross needs about eight to nine weeks of flowering to finish indoors and has a powerful narcotic buzz sure to please any indica lover.

Kings Kross

Leda Uno

According to the breeder, KC Brains in Holland, Leda Uno was created by blending KC, Brazilian, and Thai strains together. This mostly sativa hybrid has a mild lemony and minty flavor that is both refreshing and interesting. Though I would rate the potency as average at best, the creeper-type high is clear and up and has a nice smooth comedown that I wish wouldn't come quite so soon. Indoors, the plant is ready for harvest somewhere between forty-five and sixty days, depending on the phenotype chosen. Outdoors, Leda Uno can get huge, so be sure to give her plenty of space. The plant is known to be quite pest-resistant, an enormous benefit. Pictured are samples from two different growers, both grown outdoors in different parts of Mendocino, California.

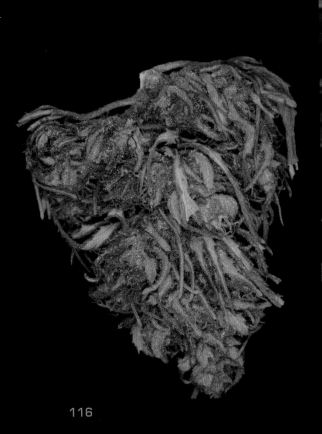

What do you get when you cross two superpotent and tasty indicas? Meet Ultimate Indica from Legends Seeds. This strain is an indica lover's dream come true. The mother used was a potent California clone known as Ortega. For the father, a second backcross of Sweet Tooth (see *Cannabible 2*, page 155) from Spice of Life Seeds was used. The end result is a head-crushing indica with extreme potency and a flavor that's pungent and skunky while at the same time sweet and funky. Traits from both parents are easily identified: The density of the buds comes from the Ortega, while the supersweetness could come only from one strain, the much-loved Sweet Tooth father. This plant, grown from seed in Northern California, grew as wide as it was tall and produced multiple pounds of fantastic herb.

Legends Ultimate Indica

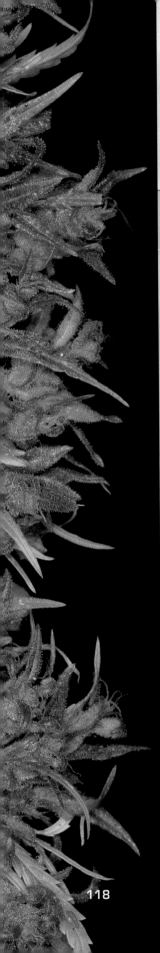

FEMINIZED SEEDS

In recent years, certain seed companies have begun selling "feminized seeds," which if made properly, grow only female plants. There is much confusion on the subject, so allow me to clarify. Feminized seeds, apparently highly beneficial to those with limited space or growing limited numbers of plants, are usually made in one of two ways. In the first method, approximately two weeks prior to flowering a female plant is treated with the substance gibberellic acid; this process is repeated when the plant begins flowering. Shortly thereafter, hermaphroditic flowers will appear on the plant, which will then pollinate itself (and any other females around), creating only female seeds. The second method involves shocking the plant by screwing with its light cycle in ways that Mother Nature never would, causing the plant to throw out hermaphroditic flowers, pollinating itself and any other female around, again creating only female seeds.

I don't recommend feminized seeds or either of these methods for the following reasons: They are very unnatural. Gibberellic acid is very toxic and nasty stuff. And, most importantly, these methods encourage hermaphroditism in the strain. I see it all the time with feminized plants. Hermies are a built-in function of the evolutionary plan, put in place to ensure the continuation of a species even in the face of massive environmental changes (read: catastrophe), which the plants might think was happening if the light started tweaking out as described.

Another thing about feminized seeds, and I know that DJ Short agrees with me on this one, is that the finished product is noticeably blander in flavor and aroma. Neither of us has yet to be impressed with feminized seeds. One possible explanation for this is that those who use feminized seeds, and those who produce them, are less likely use organic methods. The verdict: If you want all females, grow known and reputable female clones.

a hermaphrodite flower

M-1 is some kind of Kush hybrid that is sometimes seen in the California medical pot scene. The exact lineage is unknown at this time, but the unmistakable (OG) Kush flavor is there, though perhaps somewhat diluted. M-1 has a pungent and weird aroma, almost but not quite menthol tinged. The plant grows with an indica-dominant structure but isn't the typical fat main cola type. This one is short and bushy, producing even-sized buds spread over the whole plant, with no "larf." M-1 is a breeze to manicure, and many growers report favorable experiences with this heady strain. The high from M-1 is extremely powerful and sedative, requiring a nap shortly after smoking for most who partake. M-1 is to OG Kush what Granddaddy Purple is to Purple Urkel, so to speak—a more feasible commercial version of a difficult elite strain with tremendous market appeal. This sample was expertly grown outdoors organically in Northern California.

M-1

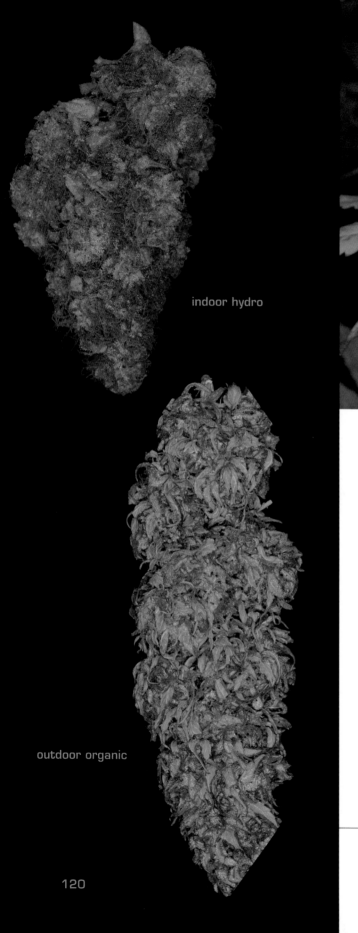

indoor hydro

outdoor organic

outdoor organic

<< M39

M39 is an old Super Sativa Seed Club (SSSC) strain that, surprisingly, is still around, albeit only in female clone form. It's a cross of a male Skunk #1 (see *Cannabible 1*, page 161) and a female Basic 5, an old Dutch commercial strain that, over the years, had proven itself valuable breeding material. The Basic 5 was described as a small and thick indica plant with a heavy, lethargic stone. When crossed with the seminal Skunk #1, a classic commercial strain was born. To this day, many a pound of M39 is grown commercially in Canada and (unfortunately) shipped to the United States. M39 is an extremely fast plant when grown indoors, harvesting average-yielding plants in under six weeks. Unfortunately, both the flavor and the high are lacking, in my opinion, leaving me craving something of much higher quality. Two samples are pictured: indoor hydro M39 (dried bud) and outdoor organic M39 (live and dried) grown in Northern California.

JK'S TOP TEN

The following are the ten strains I would want with me if stranded on a deserted island. The best I've ever smoked. The shit that tastes so good I can still remember exactly what it tastes like ten years later. This is the stuff I actually did write home about. I've organized my favorites alphabetically because at this level of quality it would be impossible to choose my absolute favorite. Most of these strains, with the exception of DJ Short's Old Time Moonshine and F-13, are low yielding and difficult to grow, and only when grown expertly do they make the cut. Also, all but the Haze, F-13, and Old Time Moonshine are clone-only females.

Asian Fantasy

Bubba Kush

The Chem/Dawg, Diesel, and OG Kush line

F-13

Haze (Metal Haze is my new favorite Haze hybrid)

HP13

Old Time Moonshine

Pure Kush

Purple Urkel

Purps

purps organic hydro

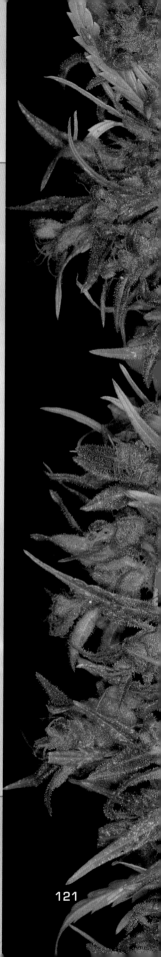

121

Malawi >>

The tiny southeast African nation of Malawi produces some of the finest cannabis on the planet. Good Malawi "cob," known to be the best herb in Africa, can be purchased for pennies in Malawi. This phenomenal sativa can stand up to any of the finest herbs being produced today in the United States or Europe. The Malawians have a special curing process that involves tightly wrapping the buds in either banana leaves or corn husks and burying them for several months. When the cobs are dug up, the herb inside has been transformed into what looks like petrified turds ranging in color from golden red to black. The banana leaves work perfectly to keep out critters while retaining the full flavor, all the while letting the whole thing breathe and ferment. From the outside, the finished product looks like corn on the cob, hence the name. I believe there's something to be said for curing in this ancient, pre–mason jar way, and I think and hope we will soon start seeing connoisseurs in these parts making their own cobs. This variety of Malawi has a golden honey-carrot flavor with a spicy haze undertone. The high is soaring cerebral sativa goodness, always edging you higher with every toke but with no burnout or cloudiness. Some people find the Malawi to be too much, causing them to feel paranoid and disoriented. These plants were grown in Northern California. Look to see locally grown Malawi in a future Cannabible, as well as complete documentation of the cob-making process.

Manga Rosa x Highland Afghani

Manga Rosa is a landrace sativa from Brazil said to have been brought by or with slaves from Angola around four hundred years ago, give or take twenty. Considering it's a pure sativa, with a flowering time of ninety days and a propensity to want to grow fifteen feet tall, **Manga Rosa** is unsuitable for indoor growing. Reeferman has taken **Manga Rosa** and crossed it with Highland Afghani (actually an F1 hybrid of two Highland Afghani cultivars that he works with), creating a hybrid with extreme vigor and flavor. The aroma of the live plant, which I photographed during a light rainstorm in Vancouver, is a sensual and tropical delight to the olfactory factory. It smells like freshly smashed mangoes and citrus and other nameless exotic and tropical fruits. The flowering time of this hybrid has been brought down and the high has much more body to it than the cerebrally pure **Manga Rosa**. The end result is a tasty and unique hybrid that will grow well indoors or outdoors.

Mango >>

KC Brains created this beautiful indica by crossing an Afghani strain with KC 33, which KC claims is an old Dutch strain blended with Thai and Brazilian genetics. Mango is very unstable, and several different phenotypes usually grow from a single pack of seeds: a lanky sativa phenotype, a bushy and compact indica phenotype, and anything in between. Luckily, some great plants usually emerge from all this variety. The aromas that some of these plants produce is fantastic, oozing of ripe mango and other tropical fruits, along with a creamy bottom end, a real nose-tickler. The indica phenotype of Mango has a murky and narcotic high, recommended for nighttime only unless you have a serious tolerance to indicas or are okay with a long daytime nap. The sativa phenotype has more of a clear and functionable high. The plants have great resin production, and some of them provide very large harvests of delicious ganja. Harvest time depends on the phenotype and ranges from forty-five to sixty-five days. Grown outdoors in Fort Bragg, California.

CLASSY GLASS 3

This mind-bogglingly beautiful and unique American art form has clearly outgrown its tiny section in the Cannabible series, so I am pleased to announce that I'm working on a book called *Heady Glass*, which will feature some of the most insane pieces ever blown. Some of these art pieces have sold for over $10,000! (Which is actually a steal considering what $10k will get you with other forms of art, like paintings.) Here is a taste. Look for *Heady Glass* sometime in 2007. Due to the recent ridiculous crack down on glass merchants, the names of the artists who created these pieces have been withheld.

The glass pinwheel actually spins as the smoke is inhaled through this sick piece.

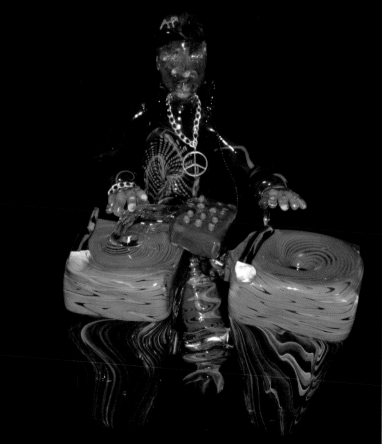

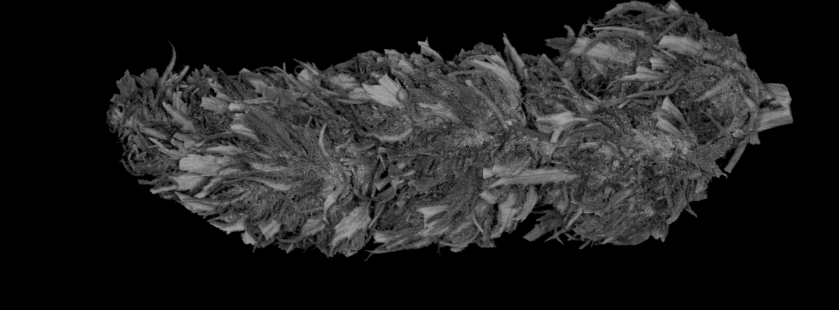

After meeting Rita Marley, Bob's wife, at the Cannabis Cup in '97, Sensi Seeds was inspired to make a strain to honor and respect the man and his message. By tinkering with several Jamaican plants they had in their mother rooms for years and blending in some fresh indica genetics, they were able to create a Jamaican sativa hybrid suitable for indoor growing. Luckily, the sample I got was grown outdoors organically in Maui, Hawaii, where the plant apparently felt right at home. The flavor, surely enhanced by its tropical organic environment, was beautiful—sweet and earthy tones of tropical deliciousness delighting my olfactory organs. The high, also undoubtedly enhanced by its tropical surroundings, was strong and thorough, and felt equally in the head and the body. As for the strain grown indoors, well, maybe in the next Cannabible.

Marley's Collie

There's no debate—this plant is gorgeous! Matanuska Tundra, a release from Sagamartha Seeds in Amsterdam, didn't even seem related to the real Matanuska Thunderfuck that I've been lucky enough to try a few times in the past. Grown outdoors in Fort Bragg, California, the plant had a really hard time, being hit with stem rot, botrytis, powdery mildew, and a variety of insects. By the time the season was over, the whole plant was basically wasted and the branches began breaking off due to its many problems. There was no mold-free sample to smoke for a report. You're better off trying to locate a clone of the real deal, in my opinion.

Matanuska Tundra

Mazar

Dutch Passion created this feminized strain by crossing an Afghani from Mazar-i-Sharif with the classic (Dutch) Skunk #1. The strain is known to be quite unstable, which can be a good or a bad thing depending on your desires. The bottom line is this: There is a lot of variation within Mazar. Several growers have also reported hermaphroditic flowers, encouraged by the feminization process, of which I am not a fan (see page 118). Though I know some people who really like Mazar, I must say the samples I smoked were not impressive. It had a slightly skunky and acrid taste, with a bit of bitterness. The high was weak and uninteresting. But I do want to mention that I know people who have picked the right pheno-type and grown Mazar indoors and been very impressed with it. I am reviewing the sample shown here, which was grown outdoors in Northern California.

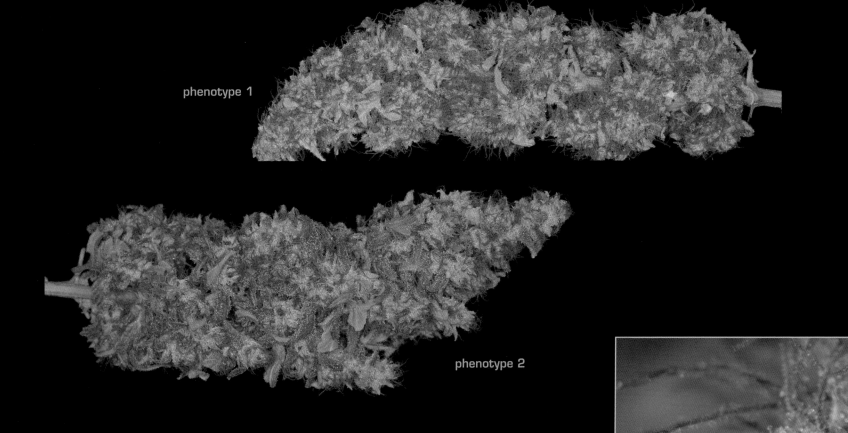

phenotype 1

phenotype 2

This strain, from Mr Nice Seeds, was originally introduced in the late 1990s as White Rhino. The heritage is Brazilian/South Indian x Afghani. Medicine Man, a close relative of White Widow, is most notable for its extremely high THC levels, easily topping 15 percent when grown well. Shantibaba, the breeder, was at the International Cannagraphic 420 Grower's Cup in 2005 and generously gave away seeds to all the winners. These plants were grown from those seeds. There are two phenotypes within Medicine Man, both indica dominant but with one showing some sativa traits. Both are extremely potent, but the one with the sativa traits has a better flavor and high, in my opinion. The flavor of Medicine Man is the best of the White line, a blend of tropical candy flavors and sweet floral tones. The strain has proven very useful to medical patients needing extremely high levels of THC. When grown indoors, the flowering time is somewhere between eight and eleven weeks, depending on which phenotype is chosen. Those that show sativa traits finish on average two weeks later than the others. Outdoors, expect the plants to finish in the beginning of October. This sample was expertly grown indoors in an organic hydroponic garden.

Medicine Man

Mekong Haze

I'm not sure what Barney's crossed into this Haze, but let me tell you, this is some trippy shit! (Barney's isn't letting out much information on this one.) Claimed to be 100 percent sativa, Mekong Haze has an incredibly earthy and rich flavor, with subtle floral tones that are evident to those who don't ruin it by mixing with tobacco. The high is visual and borderline psychedelic, a must-try for any sativa lover visiting Amsterdam. This sample, I was told, was grown indoors organically in soil.

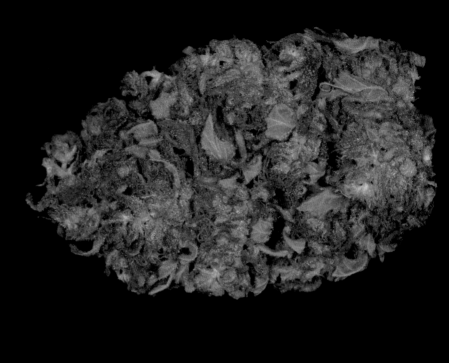

This T.H.Seeds strain is commercially viable for both the indoor and outdoor grower for several reasons. Most importantly, it produces heavy harvests of dank herb in around forty-five days indoors, finishing outdoors by the first week of September. In addition, it's a very low-odor strain, it has great resistance to pests, and it's an easy trimmer due to the very high calyx-to-leaf ratio. Mendo Madness is a cross of an old California strain known as Madness, with an extremely fast male breeder plant T.H.Seeds commonly uses. The flavor is hashy and skunky, though somewhat mild. Half a joint left me with a nice head high and a sweet skunky aftertaste. Grown outdoors in Mendocino, California.

Mendocino Madness

a moldy
spot

134

Metal Haze

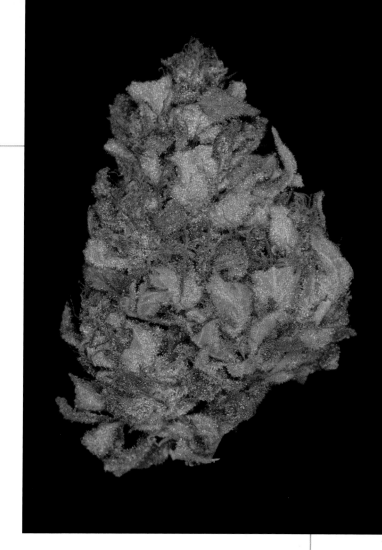

This new offering from Dutch Flowers (the seed company, not the coffeeshop in Amsterdam) is truly awesome. A gently squeezed nugget releases an olfactory explosion of natural and artificial tropical flavors reminiscent of LifeSavers candies, specifically the white piña colada, the yellow pineapple, and the pink guava. I haven't eaten artificial "foods" like these in fifteen years, but somehow I can still remember exactly what they taste like. There's also a hazy undertone—not the typical Amsterdam Haze, but some exotic new spice from outer space that words do not (yet) exist for. When smoked, the flavor is markedly different. The back of the throat is instantly coated in a thick, tangy, and pungent layer of goodness. On exhalation, the flavor is brilliantly complex and unique. Again, words do not yet exist to accurately describe it, but some that come close are pink, spicy, tropical, exotic, minty, menthol, cherry cough syrup, asafetida, putrid, and astringent. As I said, it's quite complex. The flavor continually changes throughout a joint, and all the flavors are desirable. Pungent and musty flavors that are quite delicious linger on the palate after smoking. The high from this Haze hybrid is stunning as well. A nearly debilitating euphoria, which rendered me and some friends unable to write a strain description for about twenty minutes, preceded a very strong but manageable thinking-type buzz. Great for music or art if you don't pass out in the first twenty minutes.

The lineage of Metal Haze, which was named for the metal-halide-lit room that keeps their Haze collection alive, is a sativa lover's dream come true. Dutch Flowers worked on this spectacular Haze project for many years. Males were tested the hard (and best) way—growing out their offspring to recognize the best possible pollen sources. This pollen was then used to fertilize their best Haze females. At the second generation, the offspring were heavily selected. The individuals displaying the desired potency, phenotype, flowering, and yield traits were identified and inbred into separate lines. Three years after the project began, the resulting lines were finally blended, giving rise to a hybrid that is truly spectacular. Dutch Flowers has created an incredibly potent and deliciously brain-warping Haze that is suitable for indoor growing. (Although an outdoor grown plant will blow your mind even more!) I must give praises to Dutch Flowers for this achievement. To be honest, I'm usually bored by the constant reshuffling of Dutch strains. But Metal Haze is a true breeding achievement, not the same old Dutch Haze, and sativa lovers should really check this one out. These samples were grown outdoors organically in Humboldt, California.

SHOWER CURTAIN HASH

In yet another Cannabible exclusive, I now present to you the latest advance in hash-making technology—shower curtain hash! One of my favorite growers on the planet, Shabud from Cannabis World, discovered this technique. The required tools are easy to acquire and inexpensive. You will need a large garbage can (a fifty-five-gallon olive drum works even better, as it has a lid like a mason jar and you can use the ring to hold the shower curtain and trash bag in place), an electric drill with a paint-mixer attachment, a shower curtain, a plastic trash bag, and some trim (plant matter ranging from leaf trimmings to crushed buds). Find a shower curtain made of polyester, one that if you stretch it apart while holding it up to the light you can see the small holes open up and the light shine through.

The first step is to open up the trash bag and place it in the can or drum. This makes for easy hash removal later. Then push down the shower curtain into the trash bag–lined drum to line the inside. Secure the bag and curtain in place with the ring (if it is used). Next, place one to two pounds of trim inside the can. Freezing the trim first is helpful for easier gland removal. Rapidly mix the whole thing with the drill's paint-mixer attachment. Voila! The resin glands will pass through the holes in the shower curtain while the vegetative material is held on the inside. Like any hash-making technique, the longer the material is spun, the larger the quantity but the lower the quality of the finished product—more time spinning means more time for vegetative matter to make it through the shower curtain. Less time spinning equals less hash, but it's of higher quality. After the desired amount of spinning, which should be around one to two minutes, remove the shower curtain filled with trim. The inside of the garbage bag should now be lined with sparkly resin

glands, which you can collect and press into hashish or smoke as kief.

While the finished product is clearly not as pure as well-made water hash, this technique has the water hash-making method beat on many levels. One major benefit of the shower curtain technique is that none of the terpenes (important compounds for flavor) are washed away, as invariably happens with the water technique. Another benefit over the water technique is that much larger amounts can be made at once, saving precious time. It also takes much less time than the water method, as there's no waiting period necessary. In addition, the most difficult part of making water hash, the lifting of heavy water-filled bags, is eliminated. So, to summarize, it's quicker and easier to make, larger amounts can be done at once, and sometimes even taste better.

shower diesel at 45x

Shower curtain hash made from outdoor Sour Diesel trim. A cross section reveals a fairly pure product. Not as pure as top-quality water hash, but close—and over one hundred times quicker and easier to make. The brilliant flavor of Sour Diesel is all there, having not been washed away with ice water. Water hash, aka bubble hash, can be insanely pure, but it takes about half an hour or more to make a few grams. The shower curtain method can produce a few pounds in half an hour.

MK Ultra

Anyone familiar with the legendary OG Kush strain from Southern California (see page 152) should be interested in this fine offering from T.H.Seeds in Amsterdam. Adam, the top breeder at T.H.Seeds, was able to obtain an OG Kush clone, which he then crossed with a very special G-13 cross he works with. The results are truly impressive. The brilliant OG Kush flavor is all there, yet the plant is easier to grow and quicker, and the harvest size has also been brought up to a respectable 350 grams p.s.m. (per square meter). Kudos to T.H.Seeds for making this awesome and often-hoarded strain available to the masses for a fair price. This sample was grown indoors organically in soil in Amsterdam.

Morning Glory is a Cannabis Cup–winning strain that has recently been released in seed form by Barney's Farm Seeds. Morning Glory is a cross of Breeder Steve's Sweet Tooth (see *Cannabible 2*, page 155) and Super Silver Haze (see *Cannabible 2*, page 152), two of the tastiest strains out there. The nug I scored at Barney's had an enticing musky, earthy, rich aroma, reminiscent of the Bizarre featured in *Cannabible 1* (page 39). However, the aroma didn't transition to taste very well. A joint tasted nice but not as fantastic as it smelled. This could just be a curing problem, common with Dutch herb. This was slightly disappointing, but the powerful high had my mind elsewhere fast. Morning Glory is extremely strong and narcotic, causing a pulsating buzz that I felt from my head to my toes. Perfect for a 4 a.m. jet-lag fatty!

Morning Glory

Mother's Finest >>

From Sensi Seeds comes Mother's Finest, a three-way hybrid of Haze (see *Cannabible 1*, page 84), Jack Herer (*Cannabible 1*, page 102), and a relative of Fruity Juice. Mother's Finest isn't stable, but any pack of seeds should turn up several keepers, regardless of what you're looking for. Most of the plants seem to be sativa dominant, though the occasional indica pops up, too. Winner of the 2002 Cannabis Cup for best sativa, Mother's Finest offers a wide array of flavors and highs, depending on the phenotype chosen. The Jack Herer phenotypes tend to be spicy and candied in flavor, with a speedy high. The Haze phenotypes veer more toward pine and eucalyptus with spice and a soaring cerebral high. When grown indoors, the indica phenotypes finish in around fifty days, while the sativa phenotypes can go as long as seventy-plus days. Mother's Finest is an awesome strain with amazing flavors and highs, so respect your mother!

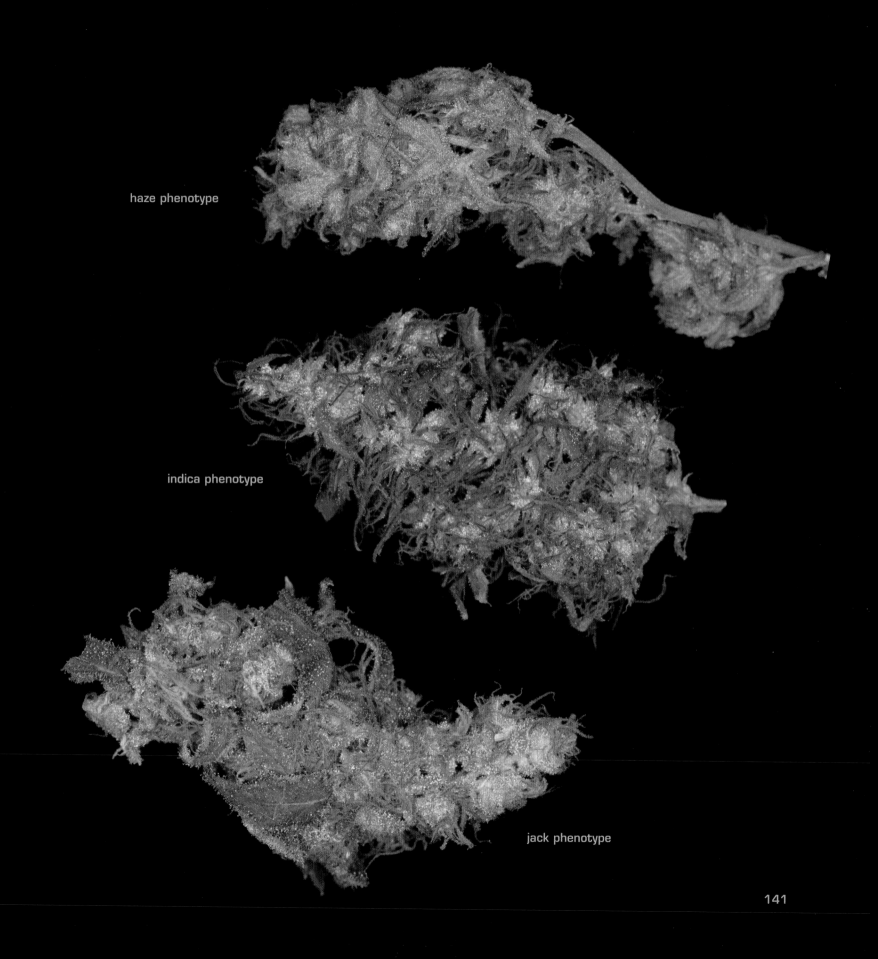

haze phenotype

indica phenotype

jack phenotype

f2

indoor organic
soil canada

indoor organic
hydro usa

<< Mountain Jam

A breeder called the Cannabis Cowboy crossed Soulshine, a potent indica that's well-known and loved in Canada, with a select DJ Short Blueberry, creating a hybrid of stunning proportions. Silky, sweet, blue, perfumey flavors with delicate spicy accents left my tongue and throat numb—literally—during and after smoking a joint. The flavor is even more amazing (and, interestingly, numbing) in a vaporizer. The high from Mountain Jam is thick and mind-warping yet somehow still functionable, a perfect blend of indica and sativa. The flowering time of Mountain Jam is seven to nine weeks, and the yields are way above average, making it well worth the wait, in my opinion. Pictured are three different samples: one grown indoors organically in soil in Canada, one grown indoors organically in a hydroponic setup in the United States, and an F2 crop (second filial generation), also grown indoors organically and hydroponically. My compliments to the breeders and the growers of this fine herb.

Mountain Mist is a heavily circulated clone in the Humboldt area of Northern California. She's mainly grown commercially, due to her bountiful and early harvest, finishing in around fifty days. Reportedly a cross of Big Bud (see *Cannabible 1*, page 35) and Afghani (see *Cannabible 1*, page 27), Mountain Mist has a pungent, fruity, and medicinal aroma, which transitions to flavor well. The high from Mountain Mist is heavy and sleepy, which some people really like. Not me. Grown outdoors organically in Humboldt, California.

Mountain Mist

WHY MOST POT SUCKS

As my appreciation for fine cannabis grows, I have become more aware of the shortcomings of most of today's herb. Upon careful examination of these short-comings, I've determined that the same four problems plague a surprisingly high percentage of today's kind bud. And it's not the genetics! Most of the strains that people grow nowadays would produce amazing medicine if grown, flushed, cured, and handled properly. This is especially sad when you consider that the hardest part is already fin-ished by the time most people screw up their crop by not properly addressing these crucial steps. After many years of paying very close attention, I have concluded that when I sample or judge any herb, the importance of these four factors means that I'm actually judging the grower more than the strain itself. Since most growers aren't address-ing these four crucial steps properly, their finished product is generally inferior to what's ultimately possible.

Growing Organically

Herb must be organically grown. In order for ganja to express its full, dazzling array of flavors and all the subtle subtones that come along with it, it simply must be grown organically. I know that many hydro growers would dis-agree with me until the end of time, but it's true. Being the author of the Cannabibles, I have been fortunate enough to sample many different growers' attempts at the same strain, even from clones, and with the exception of the Chem strain, the organic always tastes better. (For the full story of the Chem, see *Cannabible 2*, page 46.) This is not to say that properly grown hydro can't taste delicious. Sometimes it can be very delicious indeed. But that same strain grown organically will have a more diverse and satis-fying flavor, and certainly a better aftertaste.

I can understand why hydro growers were resistant to switch ten or twenty years ago—organic methods were too heavy, stinky, and messy. Luckily, this isn't the case today. Many brands of organic fertilizers and liquefied nutrients are potent and easy to use, manageable, not too messy or smelly, and affordable as well. Any good grow store should have a selection of such products. But the big reason most chemical hydro growers continue to use chemicals is because they think their bottom line—yield—would suffer by going organic. This is simply not the case. If expertly grown, organic methods will yield just as much as chemical ones, if not more. I've conducted experiments that have proven this time and time again. And even if the yield were a little less, considering that the quality is greatly enhanced, it would still be worth it. Better herb is worth more money, if that's what you're looking for.

The bottom line is this: Plants, like humans, do not want to be fed (or treated with) chemicals. A human can live (for a while) on fast food, cigarettes, and beer, but they won't thrive. It's the same with plants. Though chemically fed hydroponic plants might look healthy on the outside for a while, they aren't thriving on the inside. All the chemicals only serve to weaken the defenses of the plant, just like they do in a human. Nature's way of dealing with these weakened plants? She sends bugs, viruses, molds, and other pathogens to eliminate the weak specimens. (Survival of the fittest, remember?) Again, this is the same way it works with humans. The answer, contrary to what the chemical peddlers will tell you, is not to spray on more chemicals! You need only take a brief glimpse at what chemical agriculture has done to modern farming and farmers to understand this. Millions of acres of rich, fertile farmland have been reduced to barren, toxic, dead wasteland as a result of repeated douses with what our government calls "safe" chemicals and fertilizers. Why repeat this destructive cycle in your grow?

Consider this—one of the main techniques I use to judge herb is to roll a joint (with a Club rolling paper) and pay particular attention to the second half of the joint. This is where the true test comes in. Any decent herb can taste good on the first few hits of a joint, but it's truly special herb that tastes great right down to the last hit, with the roach burning your fingers. Most of the herb I come across tastes like hot tarry smoke by the second half of a joint, a major drawback in my book. Properly grown (and flushed!) organic herb almost always tastes great right down to the end of a joint. Chemically grown herb almost always tastes like "schwill" by the second half of a joint. Try this experiment yourself; I think you'll see what I mean. The second half of a bowl or bong load clearly reveals the benefits of organics. With chemically fed hydro, you end up with a black cruddy ball of harsh carcinogens, while properly grown organics taste delicious down to the last hit, and the residue blows away as a clean, gray ash.

Flushing

Herb must be flushed properly. This is another big one that most growers don't seem to get. In order for ganja to reach its ultimate potential quality, the plants must be cut off from food and thoroughly flushed with clean water for several weeks or more before harvest. Of course, this step is much more important when harsh chemical fertilizers are used than with organic methods. But it's necessary with any setup if you're to achieve ultimate quality. The amount of flush time varies depending on the situation, but I generally recommend stopping all feeding and switching to pure water approximately one month before harvest. This timing can be shortened for indoor plants or lengthened for outdoor plants, depending on container size, the fertilizers used, the strains grown, and a number of other factors. This gives the plant time to finish all its remaining food, at which point the leaves will start changing colors and the plant yellowing, which is part of its natural life cycle.

Yes, you might be able to crank out another few grams or so by feeding your plants up to the end or close to it, but isn't the aim for ultimate quality, not quantity? Cannabis plants that

are allowed to yellow on their path to senescence have a much more beautiful and complex flavor when smoked or vaporized than plants that are bright green right up to harvest. Again, I have done experiments that have proven this again and again. Skipping this step is one of the main factors that just about ruins most Canadian and Dutch commercial herb. (I know I will get flak for that one, but I also know that there are many connoisseurs who completely agree with me on this point!)

Curing

Herb must be cured properly. Curing is such an important step in producing fine herb but sadly is so often ignored or neglected. I believe this is because often the demand for ganja is so great that people will buy herb that hasn't been dried properly, let alone cured! Also, I think many growers are ignorant of not only the importance of this step but how to do it, as well. I am constantly amazed at how often I see herb that is genetically excellent, grown very well, harvested properly, dried properly, then sold or consumed without being cured and therefore only half as tasty as it could have been.

The curing process is quite simple: After the herb has dried to the point that a stem will snap if bent, the medicine is transferred to glass jars (preferably). (Airtight plastic containers or other clean and sealable containers can be used if the quantity is too large to jar.) Over the next couple of weeks, several times per day if possible, the jars are opened briefly. This allows the gases trapped inside the jar to escape, essentially "sweating" the nugs to golden perfection. This process also allows the last moisture hiding deep inside the buds to find its way out. During the curing process, the ganja's smell will change from a slightly vegetative stink to a near orgasmic and lusciously diverse aroma (depending on the strain of course!). Not only is the flavor greatly enhanced by curing, the high also improves. The

146

medicine will smoke better as well, burning more evenly. But most importantly, a multitude of delicious flavors that otherwise would have gone unnoticed and unappreciated will reveal themselves. One last point: Herb that has been cured properly doesn't even need to be squeezed, and therefore degraded, to smell its best. Just opening a jar of properly cured cannabis will make your mouth water!

Handling

Herb must be handled delicately. Don't even get me started on this one! Cannabis flowers are *incredibly* fragile and delicate. I cannot stress this point enough. This is the single biggest reason most pot sucks. By the time it reaches the smoker's lungs, most herb has been man-handled to the point where it is probably half as potent and tasty as it would have been if handled properly. This degradation usually starts when the plants are still alive, as people will squeeze the buds to get a smell, bump into them, drag them along the ground, and otherwise subject them to a variety of insults. During and after harvest they are manhandled even more as they are broken down, transported, hung, trimmed, moved around, dropped, and so on. Every time they're touched they degrade. It's that simple.

In order to produce what I call connoisseur-grade herb, incredible care must be taken at every single step of the process to ensure that the flowers are touched, disturbed, or molested as little as possible. This means all the way to the bong, joint, or vaporizer, where most people will roll up a little ball of herb and stick it in the bowl, getting their fingers nice and sticky in the process. That lovely smelling sticky feeling on your fingers—that's the best part of your hit, which will now be wasted. Take it from me; I spend a lot of time looking at fine canna-bis under a microscope at high magnification, so I have become hyperaware of just how delicate the flowers are, noticing how each time they're even just barely touched so many resin glands are knocked off or exploded.

And what is the first thing most people do when pack-ing a bong load? They stick their finger on it and smash it down into the bowl, even if it didn't need it, thereby remov-ing pretty much all the resin from the top (see photo). This is my pet peeve! Personally, I use scissors (always the same pair) to cut off the piece I'm going to smoke and use the metal blade to push the herb into the bowl, not letting my fingers or hands get sticky at all. Yes, you lose a little on the scissors, but at least it stays there and builds up for easy collection, which isn't the case if you use your fingers. And rolling a joint? This pretty much decimates the herb if you break it up with your (very sticky) fingers. I highly recommend the use of an herb grinder (available everywhere) for breaking up the herb. Yes, it does knock off resin, but again, it builds up inside the grinder and can be collected. As another side note, let me mention that the grower of some of the best herb in this book never touches, let alone squeezes, his flowers, and before he let me into his garden, I was told not to either! I was happy to oblige.

None of these four crucial steps adds any cost, yet they are so often skipped or neglected. It does not have to be this way. Believe it or not, most of the compressed schwaggy herb grown in Mexico, Jamaica, Africa, and many other commercial herb centers of the world would have been absolutely fantastic if you or I had harvested the plants and cared for them from that point on. Please grow or demand cannabis that is organic, flushed, cured, and handled like the delicate flower it is, and we will watch the quality of marijuana shoot way up to the highest heights on a worldwide basis! And lastly, please love your plants, as this has been proven to have a wonderful effect on plants and their growers! One Love.

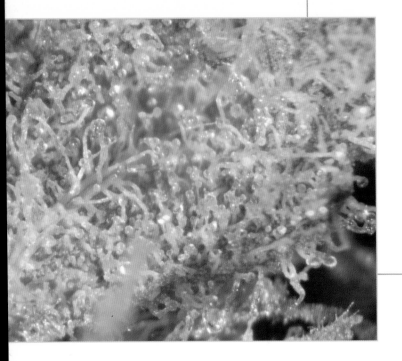

This mostly sativa strain from Paradise Seeds in Amsterdam has the typical Dutch skunky flavor with added undertones of pineapple and lime. The effects are rather heady, even soaring at times. Several different phenotypes exist within Nebula. The sativa pheno is the better one in my opinion, as it has the more pronounced tropical flavors. Paradise hasn't divulged the lineage of Nebula, but I'd guess that it's primarily made up of Skunk and White Widow genetics, with a touch of something else perhaps a little more exotic. With a flowering time of fifty-six to sixty-two days and a soaring sativa high, Nebula is a worthy strain, and I highly recommend checking it out. Grown indoors hydroponically in Amsterdam.

Nebula

Neville's Haze

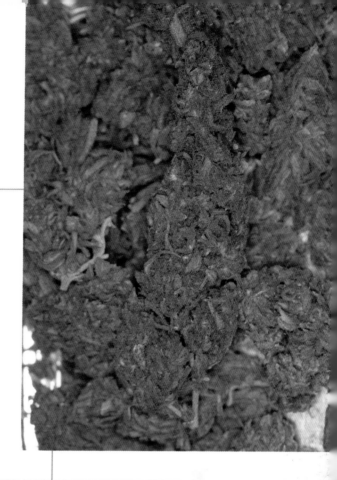

In this day and age, Neville's Haze is the closest most of us are ever going to get to smoking pure Haze, as far as I'm concerned. The lineage is listed as 75 percent Haze (see *Cannabible 1*, page 84) and 25 percent Northern Lights (see *Cannabible 1*, page 136). Some plants don't seem to have any Northern Lights in them! Neville's Haze, released by Green House Seed Company, is not for lightweights. This is seriously potent, what many would call psychedelic, herb. Known to make many hallucinate after smoking it, Neville's Haze has a soaring cerebral effect of the highest order. The flavor is a mélange of pine tree and spice, deeply earthy and satisfying. This girl takes forever to flower, twenty weeks or even longer perhaps. But if you're a sativa lover hunting out the finest sativa specimens available, this might be the one for you. Grown indoors hydroponically in Amsterdam by the man himself.

nigerian

Another of Reeferman's exotics, Nigerian Nightmare is an F1 hybrid consisting of a pure Nigerian mom blended with Afghani and Brazilian genetics. The aroma is very unique on this one, very "foody," with citrus and floral highlights. The plants are fast and fairly mold resistant, but they're also small and relatively low yielding. They finish in mid- to late September outdoors, and the finished product has a pleasant hashy flavor. Also pictured is the pure Nigerian mother used in the cross. Grown outdoors in Vancouver, Canada.

<< Nigerian Nightmare

OG Kush, aka Ogers Kush, LA Kush, Original Gangsta Kush, etc.

This legendary SoCal herb goes for as much as $8,000 a pound in L.A. It consistently fetches more than any other strain on the market. In fact, I've heard of single clones going for an astounding and insulting $20,000. Why? It's the flavor. While the high is also fantastic, the flavor of OG Kush is absolutely brilliant. It's that earthy sour, pine-cleaner, electrified-lemon, petrol flavor that has turned many a stoner in the SoCal area into a OG Kush *fiend*. As for the lineage, OG Kush is a sister to Sour Diesel, and both are descendants of the legendary Chem/Dawg-Diesel line. I don't know why they call this plant a Kush; she's obviously mostly a sativa. I don't think there's much Kush genetics in there, but the name has stuck. OG Kush is a tricky plant to grow, producing small but rock-hard nugs. She takes at least eight weeks of flowering, preferably ten if you can wait, and the harvest is modestly sized at best. All these reasons partly explain the ridiculously high prices for this herb, although it's mostly greed. The high from OG Kush is ridiculously strong, one of my favorite highs out there for sure. It's very euphoric and does the trick every time, regardless of tolerance.

152

indoor

outdoor

153

Ogre

Ogre is another West Coast clone steadfastly making her rounds. As I understand things, she's a very special Sensi Star selection. When a nug is broken up, the scent is seductively sweet. There are suggestions of tropical fruits and pine trees, with citrusy notes, a slight astringent quality, and other hard-to-describe high notes. The aroma transitions to taste adequately well. The high that **Ogre** produces is heady and quite lengthy as well. Cerebral in nature, it reflects the sativa genetics. Grown indoors organically in soil.

ELITE CLONE LIST

Nearly two hundred spectacular clone-only strains are being kept in and traded only around North America. Known as "elites" due to the fact that they are highly sought after, very hard to obtain, and incredibly special, they are the best of the best. It is interesting to note that very few of these clones have ever made it to Amsterdam or even Canada.

"Elite clones" are very special individual female plants that various different growers discovered and kept alive in clone form: One special phenotype saved and passed on for her special qualities. This list is by no means complete and it grows all the time, but these are some of the best out there that I know of. How many have you tried?

Bubblegum	G-13	M39
Bullrider	Garlic	Manic
Bwanana	Ginger Ale	Mass. Super Skunk
Cafe Girl	Genius	Matanuska Thunderfuck
Cali-O Sativa	God	Millies
Catpiss	Golden Goat	Mothership
Champagne	Golden Haze	MSM's Mr Nice
Cheese	Granddaddy Purple	NorCal Cript
Chem/Dawg	Grape Ape	OG Kush
Chemo	Grapefruit	Old Blue
Cherry Bomb	Gravity	Orange Friesland
Cherry Slyder	Green Crack (same as Cush)	Oregon Funk
Chocolate Thai	Grimm White Widow	Oregon Purple Thai
Chocolate Trip	Hash Plant #1	Ortega
Coral Reef	Hawaiian Webbed Indica	P91
Corn	Herijuana	Pacific G-13
Cotton Candy Kush	High Octane	Pez
Cough #1	Hogsbreath	Pineapple Thai
Cough #2	HP13	Pine Bud
Crazy Train	Humboldt Snow	Pink Kush
Cuddlefish Hash Plant	Jacki-O	Princess
Cush (same as Green Crack)	Jack's Cleaner	Pukeberry
Dabney Blue	Jedi	Pure Kush
Dank Ass Bitch	Killer Queen	Purple Indica
DHK's Black Domina	King Kush	Purple Kush
Diesel	Kong	Purple Urkel/Urple
Dogshit	Kryptonite	Rene
Dumpster	Krystal Spike	Romulan Joe Indica
Durban Thai Highflier	Lemon Bomb	Romulan Joe Sativa
Elvis	Lemon G	Rotten Kush
Emerald Triangle	Lemonaid	*(continued)*

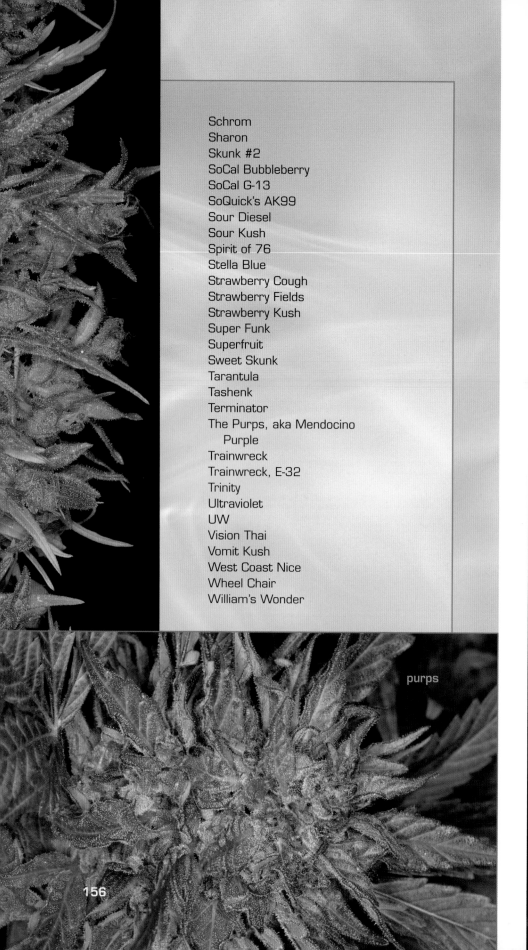

purps

156

indoor
organic
hydro

<< Old Time Moonshine

organic
hydro

It is very rare that I come across a new strain that blows me away. This happened instantly the first time I tried Old Time Moonshine (OTM), one of DJ Short's new strains. Old Time Moonshine is a true Hash Plant, and a unique one at that. OTM was selected for its production of large, clear gland heads, as clearly seen in the microscope photo. But what got me about this strain is the flavor. It's unbelievably complex, and hard to describe as well. It hits on all sorts of crazy high notes ranging from Lebanese hashish to spicy aftershave. The bottom end has a luxurious musky tone that puts a bizarre twist on the flavor. Exhalation brought a huge smile to my face every time in appreciation of the strength and earthy uniqueness of the flavor. The high from OTM is powerful and unique as well. It's definitely in the couchlock category, yet it is somehow clear as well. No muddy mental state as is so often the case with most of today's indicas. Kudos to DJ Short for his fine selecting skills! OTM harvests in seven to eight weeks indoors, mid-September outdoors. Yields are above average, and please be aware that Old Time Moonshine was a limited release, so find it if you can! Grown indoors organically and hydroponically.

indoor
organic
soil

organic outdoor

Petrolia Headstash 2

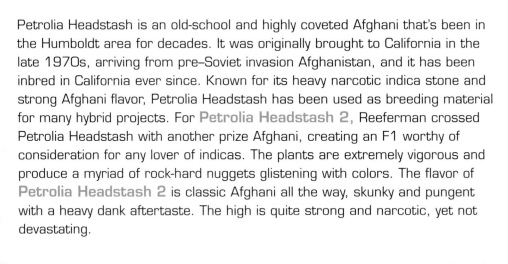

Petrolia Headstash is an old-school and highly coveted Afghani that's been in the Humboldt area for decades. It was originally brought to California in the late 1970s, arriving from pre–Soviet invasion Afghanistan, and it has been inbred in California ever since. Known for its heavy narcotic indica stone and strong Afghani flavor, Petrolia Headstash has been used as breeding material for many hybrid projects. For **Petrolia Headstash 2,** Reeferman crossed Petrolia Headstash with another prize Afghani, creating an F1 worthy of consideration for any lover of indicas. The plants are extremely vigorous and produce a myriad of rock-hard nuggets glistening with colors. The flavor of **Petrolia Headstash 2** is classic Afghani all the way, skunky and pungent with a heavy dank aftertaste. The high is quite strong and narcotic, yet not devastating.

Pineapple Mist >>

This is a canna-project that some ambitious breeders in the Humboldt area are working on. It's a cross of Pineapple (see *Cannabible 2*, page 126) and Matanuska Mist (see *Cannabible 2*, page 96). Work is currently being done to stabilize the line. The sample I got leaned more toward the Matanuska Mist, evident by the powerful narcotic stone and mild, unexciting flavor. The breeders and I prefer the more Pineapple-like plants because their flavor is much more tropical and enticing. Also pictured is Purple Pineapple Mist, which has Urkel crossed into the mix.

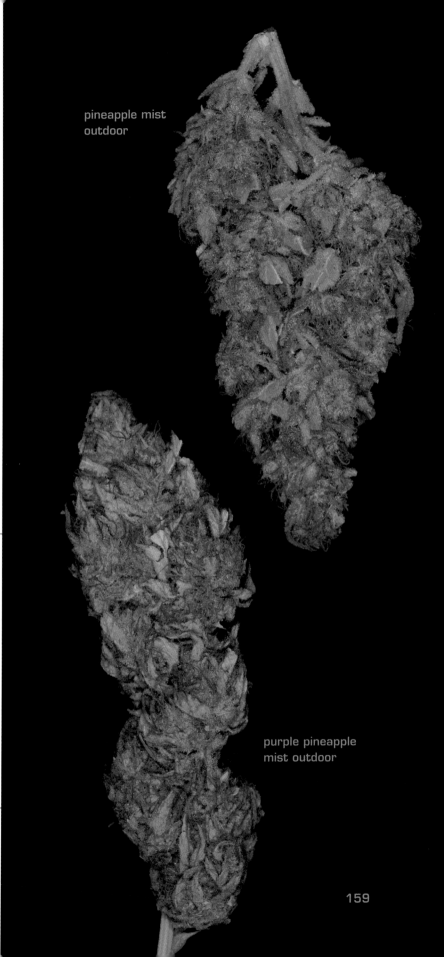

pineapple mist
outdoor

purple pineapple
mist outdoor

159

pinetar kush x
mexican

Pinetar Kush

Coming from a breeder known as Tom Hill, **Pinetar Kush** is an inbred line from Pakistan that I photographed while hunting dank in Humboldt, California. The plant is a pure indica and a relatively prolific producer of skunky, piney nuggets. I found the high rather up for an indica, but the potency was mild. The flavor is lemon-lime pine, though not very strong. The plants are hardy and mold resistant and finish in early October outdoors, while indoors they take about sixty days. Also pictured is Pinetar Kush crossed with a Mexican sativa. Grown in a greenhouse in Humboldt, California.

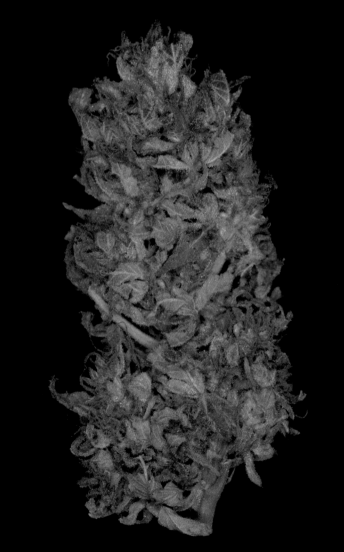

160

ARE YOU SIRIUS?

Take a look at the word *cannabis*. Ever wonder what it means? Cannabis is a Greek word, though its root is African. In Greek, *canna* means "canine," or "dog," and *bis* or *bi* is the number two. So cannabis is the "two dog plant"! That in itself is interesting to me. But the pot thickens.

There is a cannabis-loving tribe in Mali, West Africa, called the Dogon tribe. A fairly well-documented group, the Dogons were visited by Herodotus, a Greek traveler and chronicler, around 300 BCE. He was fortunate enough to have visited the Dogons during a yearlong celebration (makes the Cannabis Cup seem pretty weak!) that took place every fifty years. Explaining their celebration, the Dogons pointed to the brightest star in the winter sky, Sirius, and said it was the "Two Dog Star," and that it was the home of the "two dog plant," cannabis. The two dog plant, they said, was brought to our planet by the goddess from the Two Dog Star. Their yearlong celebration was in honor of that star.

All of this would be easy to dismiss if not for the fact that the Dogons possessed specific knowledge about the Sirian system for thousands of years before scientists with modern telescopes and equipment could catch up and prove them right. The Dogons had specific knowledge about Sirius B, a white dwarf star, which they call Po Tolo. They knew that it was white, that it was extremely small, and that it was the heaviest star in its grouping. (As it turns out, it's three hundred times denser than diamonds.) They were able to describe its elliptical orbit with Sirius A, its fifty-year orbital period, and the fact that the star rotated on its own axis. Sirius B is invisible to the naked eye and is so difficult to observe, even through a telescope, that no known photographs were taken of it until 1970.

They also described a third star in the Sirius system, which they called Emme Ya. In 1995, when two French astronomers published the results of a multiyear study of what was apparently a small, red dwarf star within the Sirius star system, the Dogon idea of there being a Sirius C, aka Emme Ya, was suddenly taken much more seriously. If the Dogons were correct in all of their other knowledge about Sirius, why would they not be dead on

with their claims of cannabis being from Sirius? It is, after all, named after that Two Dog Star!

Think about it: The Dogons were celebrating the fifty-year orbital period of the Sirius system for thousands of years before astronomers could even detect Sirius B. How did they know this? The Dogons claim that their astronomical knowledge was given to them by the Nommo, amphibious beings sent to earth from Sirius for the benefit of mankind.

Could all of this potentially explain the astounding diversity within the cannabis gene pool? Speaking specifically to flavors, there are cannabis strains with flavors ranging from the sweetest fruit all the way to foul rotten meat (in a good way, if that is somehow possible!)—from astringent pine cleaner to chocolate to kids' vitamins. I've tasted ganja strains that mimicked every fruit on the planet, including strawberry, grape, peach, lemon, lime, plum, raspberry, blueberry, guava, blackberry, mango, cherry, orange, banana, pineapple, melons, and more. I've also tasted flavors reminiscent of just about every herb used in cooking, including mint, basil, sage, rosemary, and thyme. This amazing variety of familiar flavors is well documented in the Cannabible series, but you may have noticed that on occasion I find myself at a loss for words when providing tasting notes. There we enter the realm of all the outer space flavors that words do not exist for, because there are no other similar flavors found on earth, and thus no accurately descriptive words. I find that about half of the really good strains out there have these otherworldly flavors.

What if these strains and flavors really are from outer space? What if cannabis is a plant highly regarded and traded not just on our planet, but throughout the universe? I picture cannabis as a miraculous plant that grows on thousands of planets throughout the universe and is introduced to suitable planets by benevolent beings, such as the Nommo, to help "spread the love." Are you with me?

Note: The Dog Star was highly venerated in ancient Mesopotamia, where its old Akkadian name was Mul-lik-ud (Dog Star of the Sun), and in Babylonia, where it was called Kakkab-lik-ku (Star of the Dog). The Assyrians called Sirius Kal-bu-sa mas (the Dog of the Sun), and in Chaldea, it was known as Kak-shisha (the Dog Star That Leads).

<< PK (Pure Kush)

Arguably the rarest and most expensive elite ganja strain on the planet, PK, local to Southern California, sells for a mind-boggling $1,000 an ounce to those rich or crazy enough to buy it (mostly movie stars and other rich Hollywood types). Most of the true connoisseurs I know have never even heard of it, let alone tried it. In fact, it took me several months to acquire this sample, a half an eighth (1.75 grams) that sold for an astounding $65. The strain is primarily found in Los Angeles and surrounding areas, and there are a few cannabis buyers clubs that stock it from time to time. PK is difficult to grow, the yield is small, and the wait is long—seventy days of flowering time is required to finish. So you can see that from the grower's perspective, they're not price gouging as much as it may seem. The same grower could grow a commercial strain that's twice as heavy and twice as fast, making even more money than if they grew PK and sold it for $1,000 an ounce. Please make no mistake: I am not excusing these prices—they are ridiculous and insulting. I'm just trying to paint a clear picture of what it takes to grow this strain commercially.

PK is a specialty item, an exquisite treat for the rich and famous (or at least the rich). It has an awesome aroma, almost identical to Froot Loops cereal but with an intense Kushy bottom end. The aroma transitions to taste beautifully, and an intense buzz comes on even before the smoke is exhaled. The stuff expands like a neutron bomb exploding in your lungs, leaving all but the most hard core in a coughing fit. Once the high fully hits, the strain's elite status begins to make sense. PK is incredibly strong, producing a throbbing buzz felt emanating from the heart outward. The high is very euphoric, and long-lasting as well. I was still thoroughly baked four hours after smoking it. Though, to be honest, I wouldn't necessarily rate the strain as any better than expertly grown Diesel, Sour Diesel, Chem/Dawg, OG Kush, or some of the other elite clones that make their way around Southern California and other locales. In fact, PK is very similar to Chem/Dawg, and I wouldn't be surprised if they were closely related. A lot of hype definitely surroundes this strain. This batch was grown with chemicals in a hydroponic setup, and the quality definitely suffered as a result. No doubt the strain would be much better if grown organically. Many thanks to the brother who donated this to the cause.

Platinum

Platinum is supposedly a Blueberry selection, though it seems barely, if at all, related. It came from Michigan and eventually made its way to Northern California, where, due to its flowering period of only forty-two days, it's currently being grown as a commercial strain. Some growers choose to let Platinum go fifty to fifty-six days, but any longer is too much. At sixty days, mold may become an issue due to increasing density, lack of growth, and overall weakening functions. Platinum clearly demonstrates its indica-based heritage by being relatively bland in flavor and thoroughly narcotic in effect. Not necessarily a connoisseur's delight, but extremely functional in the garden. Grown indoors organically in soil.

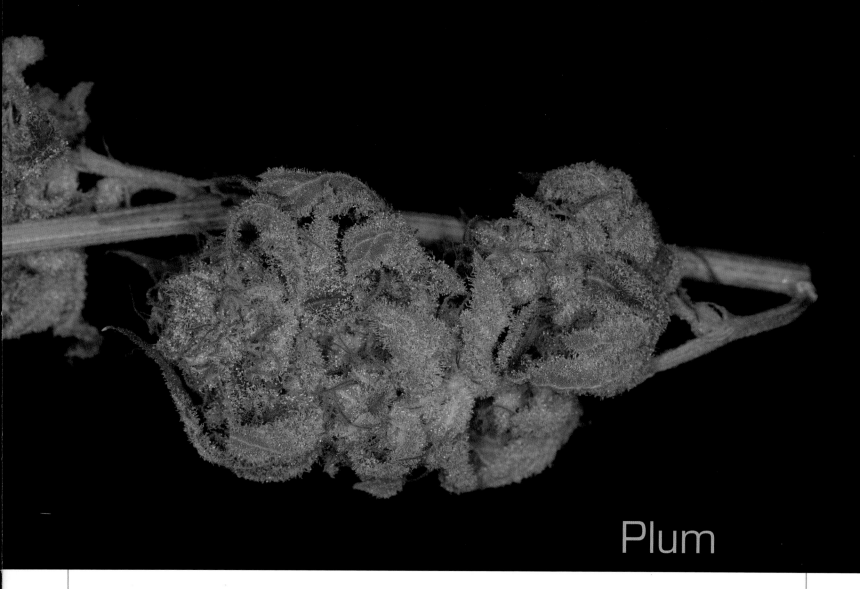

Plum

Plum is an old Spice of Life strain (1994) that a few heads here and there are still growing, luckily! It's a cross of Big Skush and a very special Blueberry male. Big Skush was made by crossing a Sensi Big Bud x Skunk #1 with a strain being called "Kush," which, according to Breeder Steve, was really more of a South Indian sativa. The Blueberry father was interesting in that it had "chromatic resin," which looked like little metallic ball bearings all over its tight stamen clusters. This was the same male used in many of Spice of Lifes's strains, including Sweet Tooth (see *Cannabible 2*, page 155), Shishkeberry, and Blue Domino. The thing that's so amazing about the Plum bud is the flavor. It's wonderfully delicate and spicy, with sumptuous candy plum tones that I've not noticed in any other strain. The high from Plum is top-notch—warm, heady, and very strong but not in a devastating way. It's more introspective and thought-provoking. Plum is a very flexible, vinelike plant. This plant is reluctant to let dead leaves fall off, a peculiarity which can encourage mold. The solution is to manually clean the plants as they grow—an extra step, but worth it for bud of such exquisite quality. Look for a rerelease of the Plum bud soon (if all goes well).

PMS >>

We all know that cannabis can be extremely helpful to women with PMS, as well as their mates. This fact has now been commemorated in cannabis history with an honorary strain, **PMS**, or Pineapple (see *Cannabible 2*, page 126) x Mothership (see *Cannabible 2*, page 110). A very special Pineapple male was crossed with the highly coveted Mothership female, and a truly medicinal strain was born. Mothership is an exotic sativa that was all the rage in Ashville, North Carolina, for most of the 1990s, until, due to strain-hoarding, it was lost. (Don't bogart the genetics!) Luckily, someone rescued her and headed west to California, where she is much happier growing in the full California sun. When crossed with the famous Pineapple strain from California, full hybrid vigor was achieved and an incredibly delicious strain emerged. **PMS** has a complex flavor that hits everything from sweet-sappy-tropical to dank-pungent-limy. It's especially tasty in fatty form, where the flavor seems to get better and better until your lips are burnt on the roach. The high is giggly and happy, and lengthy as well. Grown outdoors organically in Mendocino, California.

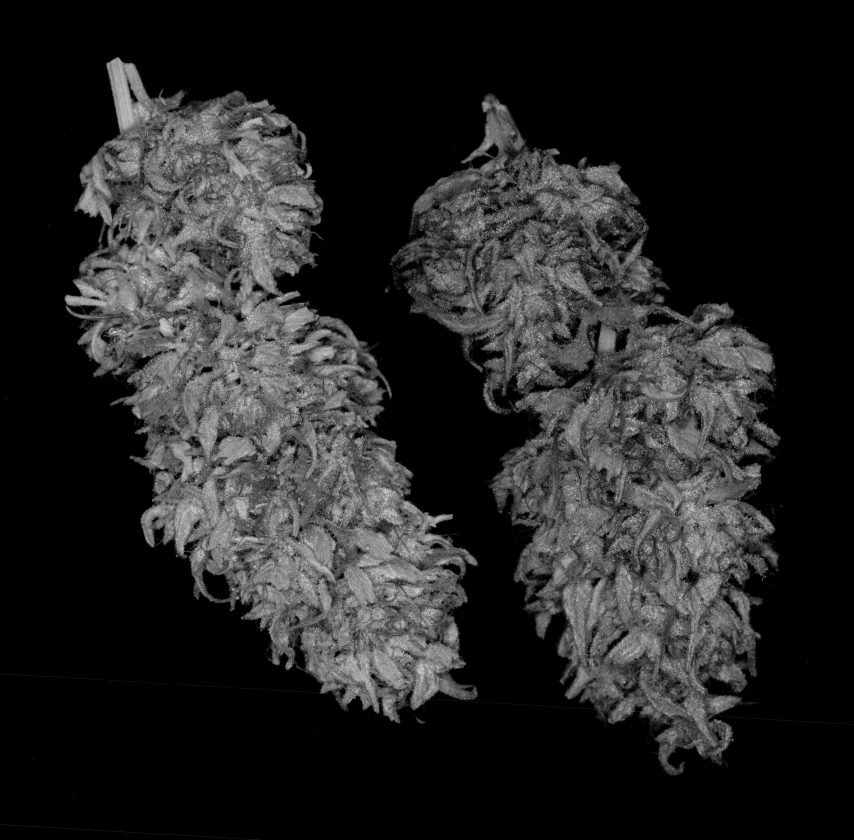

Here we have a blend of two of the most common strains in Amsterdam, Hindu Kush (see *Cannabible 1*, page 89) and Skunk #1 (see *Cannabible 1*, page 161). Flying Dutchmen Seeds, creators of many fine cannabis strains, have released **Pot of Gold** in seed form. The plants have your standard Dutch sweet and skunky aroma, pleasant but nothing new. The buzz is mellow and spacey, a little generic for my personal tastes. Grown indoors in soil in Amsterdam.

Pot of Gold

Purple #1 >>

Notable for its extreme purple coloration and not much else, Purple #1 is a seed strain available from Dutch Passion Seed Company. A hearty plant that balances out at 50 percent indica and 50 percent sativa, Purple #1 has a mild high (almost unnoticeable to me) and a rough, lightly sweet flavor that I did not cherish. The plants are well suited to outdoor growing in Holland or other cold and wet climates where not much else will grow successfully. Grown outdoors in Northern California.

outdoor organic

indoor organic soil

Purple Indica

This pure indica clone, which originally came from Seattle, was expertly grown outdoors organically in the Sacramento area. Purple Indica is to Seattle what Diesel is to New York. The flavor of Purple Indica is fantastic, a spicy candied purple perfumey assault on the taste buds that puts a giant grin on the face every time. There is a pronounced astringent quality to the smoke, as well as a taste of something resembling anise. She's one of the better-tasting purple strains going around, perhaps only bested by the Purps and well-grown Purple Urkel. The high from Purple Indica reminded me of Herijuana. It's insanely potent, with a heavy, lethargic, and sometimes throbbing buzz that puts me down for a nap every time. Watch out for extreme munchies with this strain! Not my favorite daily smoker, but a very tasty occasional treat. Also pictured is a nug grown indoors organically in soil, which was also awesome.

172

Purple Kush

This is the main **Purple Kush** clone currently grown in California. This gorgeous indica packs a wallop of a narcotic buzz, a true Kush to say the least. The flavor is exquisite—not as tasty as the Mendocino Purps but excellent nevertheless. It really tastes like purple candy, along with hints of sandalwood, musk, sage, and other earthy notes. This one fetches $500 to $800 per ounce in the L.A. Kush market. The plant is a moderate yielder at best. (Why does it seem like the best plants are almost always the low yielders?) Grown indoors organically in soil.

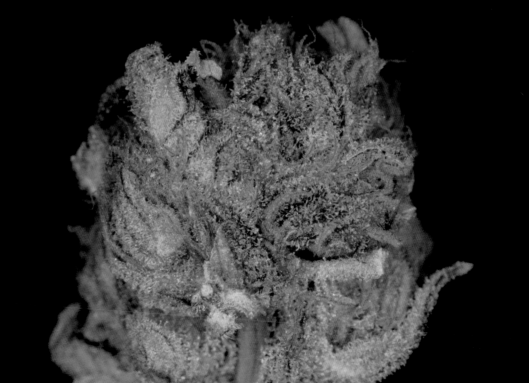

SEED KNOCKOFF COMPANIES

I've said it before, and I'll say it again: The seed business is very seedy. There's a new trend within this industry that warrants discussion, and this trend is seed knockoffs. Different levels of seed knockoffery exist, but the worst kind, and what this piece is about, is when a company gets a pack or so of seeds from a reputable strain (that someone else worked on, possibly for years), crosses their choice of the best male and female, and sells the seeds (F2s) under the same name—sometimes for more than the original breeder charges! This is theft, plain and simple. In the world of (legal) commercial agriculture, a swift lawsuit would end this venture and award monetary compensation to the original breeder or copyright owner. But considering that marijuana is illegal in most of the world, there is little if anything that the original breeder can do about it. Some companies, including Sensi Seeds in Holland, trademark the names of their strains. However, enforcing these trademarks can be somewhat of an impossibility due to the illegal nature of the plant.

Also of interest is that the F2s that these knockoffers produce usually are extremely unstable, to the point where many buyers don't even find one keeper in the plants produced by a pack of seeds. Often these knockoffs even damage the reputation of the real breeder, as many knockoff consumers don't even know they got knockoffs (or what a knockoff is!), and most if not all knockoffs are inferior to the original material. So a person can go buy some Sensi Star knockoff seeds, for example, and due to the poor selection skills of the knockoff artist, end up with some mediocre herb. They will then assume (and tell others) that Sensi Star was unimpressive, when the truth is that Sensi Star is wonderful but they bought some crappy knockoff seeds.

On another level, some people claim that low-priced knockoffs can be a good thing because they allow many more growers, some of whom cannot afford to spend $300 on a pack of seeds from the original seed bank, to access the best genetics. I don't agree with this. In my view, a pot grower can't afford *not* to buy the best seeds available. With pot prices as high as they are—good herbs costing more than gold—a seed investment is minimal and cutting corners is a bad idea. Although $300 won't buy even an ounce of top-quality herb, it will buy you the genetics that can produce an endless amount of top-quality herb. Nothing is more important than your seed choice, and most or all of the knockoffs are inferior—distant, weak cousins of the real deal.

As with anything in life, there's an honorable way to do things and a dishonorable way. To take other people's various strains, work with them to make crosses, and sell them as what they actually are—a cross of strain A and strain B, selected for characteristic C—is fine in my book. As an example of the highest form of this, let's look at Blue Satellite. Breeder Steve crossed one of his own strains, Shishkeberry, with DJ Short's Blueberry. They privately reached a fair arrangement, and Steve gives full credit to DJ Short in his strain description. This is a fair and honorable situation and not a knockoff at all. Disclosure is the key issue here. Anything beyond this gets shady. If knockoff F2s are made, the seller should at the very least give credit to the original breeder and identify the seeds as F2s. In a closer-to-perfect world, they should also compensate the original breeder, in my opinion. Unfortunately, this rarely, if ever, happens. After years of having their own strains knocked off in every way possible, Sensi Seeds has now started White Label, their own knockoff line. If you can't beat 'em, join 'em is the philosophy, I guess.

The bottom line is that the educated cannabis consumer should do some research before choosing a seed strain to purchase. The online community has been a great help in identifying the scammers. I highly recommend going online (try overgrow.com or cannabis world.com) and doing a search on the seed bank you're considering ordering from. See what other people have to say about the company. What are you looking for? Just one good mother or a stable, homogenous line? Breeding material? Or perhaps a relatively uniform crop to grow from seed? And here's the big one: Who do you want to support?

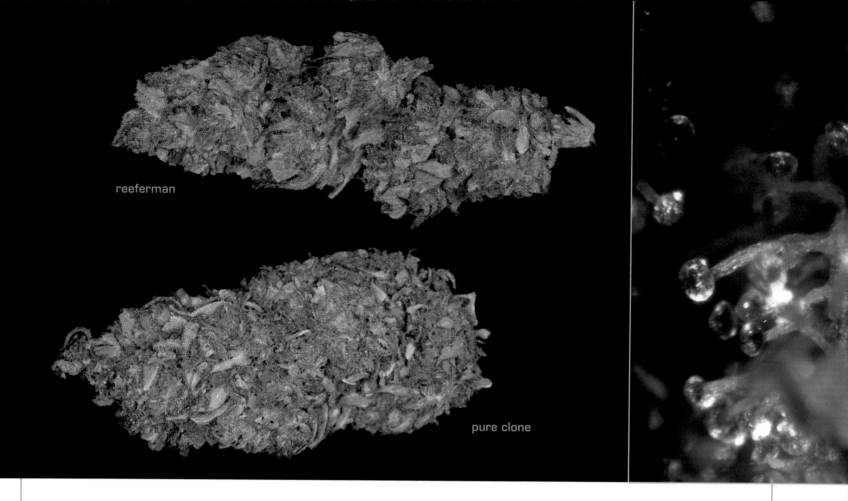

reeferman

pure clone

Purple Pineberry is a clone-only strain commonly grown outdoors in Canada. Due to her hardiness, large harvests, mold resistance, and early finishing time, in recent years she has become the number one outdoor Canadian strain grown for export to the United States. Several seed companies sell a hybrid of Purple Pineberry, including Reeferman, Green Life Seeds, and Secret Valley Seeds. All were crossed with different males, and they vary in quality. The pure clone is what I'm reviewing here. This strain is very well named—it really tastes like purple, pine, and berries. The cured finished product smells a bit like Trainwreck, earthy and spicy and extremely aromatic, with additional piney and purple tones. It reminds me of old-school top-quality Columbian herb. The high from Purple Pineberry is nice at first, though a tolerance quickly builds to this strain. The effects can be a bit cloudy, but if you get a good batch of Pineberry the high can be felt from head to toe, radiating from the third eye outward. Grown outdoors organically in British Columbia. My compliments to the growers: This was the best Canadian export I've ever tried (the deliverer of the herb did not admit that it came from B.C. until I asked several times, having had a strong suspicion). I should also mention that this was by far the best of about ten different batches of Purple Pineberry that I have come across. Many of the others were pretty terrible, mostly due to rough outdoor growing seasons in B.C. Also pictured is a bud of Reeferman's Purple Pineberry.

Purple Pineberry

Purple Power

Several seed companies sell a strain called **Purple Power**, including Nirvana, and Female Seeds. All of them are variations of the same strain, which is actually comprised of Thai and Columbian genetics crossed with a very early Dutch Skunk. Make no mistake about it, this is an outdoor strain. Most notable for its deep purple coloration, **Purple Power** is hearty enough to handle some northern climates, finishing around mid-September. The smoke is nice, though perhaps a bit rough and certainly not the best out there. It's slightly spicy, slightly sweet, and earthy. The high is mild and clear, perfect for lightweights but weak to spoiled people such as myself. Grown outdoors organically on the West Coast.

This hybrid was just so beautiful I had to include it. Coming from a company known as East Island Seeds, **Purple Skunk x Dutch Treat** is fairly unstable, so expect variation from a pack of seeds. The right phenotype will not only be purple and stunning to look at, it will also have a lovely hashy, skunky, and citrusy flavor. Indoors she likes to go sixty-five days, while outdoors expect harvest to come by mid-October. The high is medium in strength and balanced nicely, somewhat heady but still with a euphoric edge. Grown outdoors in Fort Bragg, California.

Purple Skunk x Dutch Treat

I photographed these stunning specimens while visiting Reeferman in British Columbia. A new strain is his line, **Purple Thunder,** a cross of Kodiak Gold (Lavender phenotype) and Early Durban (Afghani x Durban), which was the father. Three different phenotypes can easily be identified, each one more beautiful than the last. The buds on this strain are especially dense, yet they're also known to be mold resistant. The aroma is simply intoxicating, a purple perfumey hashish assault on your olfactory senses with tinges of mint and anise. The plants finish in late September outdoors. The high is powerful and up, great for being high but still getting things accomplished. Grown outdoors on Vancouver Island.

Purple Thunder

178

hydro

outdoor humboldt

indoor organic soil

180

The Urkel is a clone that is now extremely popular on the West Coast, especially in the more popular buyers clubs. The Urkel is always a pleasure to smoke, and it's truly one of my favorites. The flavor is fantastic, a velvety and robust candied purple thing with heavy hints of cardamom. The high is extremely strong, a head-throbbing, pulsating buzz that might be too much for some lightweights. Definitely night-time herb. Some have claimed that Urkel is actually from Lavender seed stock. The Urkel is tricky to grow, and yields are modest at best, with most indoor growers getting about a half pound per 1,000-watt light. This helps explain the high prices the strain usually fetches. One notable characteristic of **Purple Urkel** is that a joint always tastes great until the very end, regardless of who grew it. Pictured are three versions: indoor hydro, indoor organic soil, and outdoor organic from Humboldt, California.

Purple Urkel

outdoor organic

indoor organic soil

181

CANNABIS BUYERS CLUBS

Ever since the passage of Proposition 215, which legalized medical marijuana in California (at least on a statewide level), there has been a proliferation of cannabis buyers clubs (CBCs, or compassion centers, co-ops, dispensaries, or health centers) opening in many cities, particularly on the West Coast. The shops range from dingy and shady hole-in-the-wall dives to modern, well-lit, beautiful, and consciously run establishments set up to help sick people. It seems as though more lean toward the former. Going into a CBC for the first time can be a very strange experience. One is overwhelmed with the feeling of "Holy shit! Am I in the United States?" Due to the shaky legal ground the clubs operate on, raids are not uncommon. Armed robberies also happen from time to time, so be aware of the safety levels of the various clubs if you choose to go. Some of the better clubs offer their patients extras like deliveries, yoga classes, snacks, vaporizers, massage, and other healing modalities.

The opening of these clubs, some of which sell many pounds daily, has changed the entire herb market on the West Coast. Most of the clubs have doctors they work with who assist patients and make recommendations. Many of the clubs stock a vast assortment of ganja, often more than thirty strains, as well as ten or more types of hashish or other concentrates—more selections than most coffeeshops in Amsterdam have, to put it in perspective. A good number of shops also sell cannabis edibles, ranging from cookies and chocolates to ganja lollipops.

As in Amsterdam, most of the buds sold in CBCs are commercially grown and lack the quality that the discerning connoisseur seeks, although there are definitely exceptions. The prices, unfortunately, are usually high, with the average eighth (3.5 grams) of what they call top-quality herb selling for $55 to $65—more than most people pay on the black market! Some clubs in Southern California sell eighths

all day long of certain elite strains (OG Kush, Pure Kush) for $100. I guess the people who run these clubs think, "Good thing most sick people are also millionaires!" Average-quality herb is usually about $40 to $45 for an eighth in most clubs. Top-quality water hash often tops $55 a gram. There are several reasons for the high prices. Although greed is most often the driving force, another reason, at least in some of the nicer clubs, is the high overhead associated with running a good club. A large number of employees, as well as a security force, are usually necessary—things a black market dealer doesn't have to pay for.

Currently, some of the more popular strains in the Bay Area clubs are Purple Urkel, Trainwreck, Purps, OG Kush, and Blue Dot. Many shops make up their own names for strains, confusing things for the customer and making my work more difficult. Often a strain that isn't selling well is renamed to move it out. The bottom line is this: Whether you call them coffeeshops or a cannabis buyers clubs, places where people can purchase their medicine in a safe environment are needed. For this reason alone, I am in favor of the clubs operating. I do, however, wish their buyers would be more discriminating and their prices would be lower. That said, these clubs are a huge step toward the full legalization of marijuana in the United States.

super silver haze dipped in
super silver haze honey oil >>

183

Pursang Haze

I picked up this superfruity nugget at Barney's in Amsterdam. I was told that it was a cross of Jack Herer (see *Cannabible 1*, page 102) and Super Silver Haze (see *Cannabible 2*, page 152). Sounds believable, though I would have thought it to be spicier. No spice here, just an overpowering fruitiness, not so much one specific fruit but more like fruit punch. Also present is a background astringent characteristic and perhaps a tease of anise. As for the high, no lack of potency here! This herb is happy, giggly stuff, and quite cerebral as well. Recommended for any sativa lover visiting Amsterdam. Grown indoors in soil.

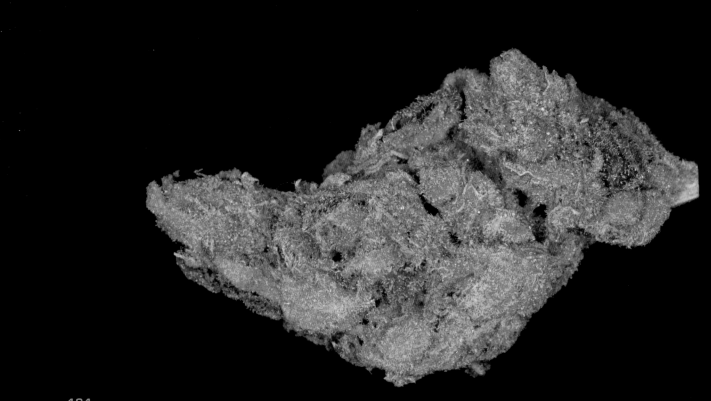

Rene >>

Rene is a Canadian clone-only strain that is well loved by the lucky few who still have access to her. Said to have originated in Montreal and thought to be named after her breeder, Rene eventually made her way west to Vancouver, where she still resides. Unfortunately, she's getting tired in her old age (after too many clones from clones, the genetic information has thinned out too much), so now she's being bred with some fresh genetic material to revive her (see Highend, page 109). As for the pedigree details, Rene is said to be a cross of a female Himalayan sativa with a male Skunk #1. Rene is a seriously pungent plant (she gets that from daddy), possessing a quality that Bubbleman and I refer to as "the Funk." It's hard to describe, it's just that funky thing that several other elite strains also have, including Sour Diesel, HP13, OG Kush, Chem/Dawg, and so on. This girl is sometimes known as "pot to get you busted" due to her seemingly uncontrollable odor. Rene has a wonderful high, cerebrally active and very up. Pictured are two samples of pure Rene, still amazingly kick-ass considering the weakening of the mother plant. A fresh sample and a well-cured sample, both grown indoors organically in soil, are pictured.

fresh sample

cured sample

S 1 5

Sweet Skunk was blended with a five-way cross of Afghani #1, Northern Lights, Haze, Hindu Kush, and Skunk #1 to create this canna-mutt known as S 1 5. This is a plant of serious girth, often needing a little help holding itself up due to the large colas. S 1 5 is now a clone-only strain that's commonly grown in Northern California. The aroma of the live plant is classic skunk with fruity and floral tones. The dried bud is not extremely flavorful, though it's not bad either. S 1 5 has good commercial appeal, as it's a very heavy producer and finishes relatively quickly: in about seven weeks indoors, in late September outdoors. The high from S 1 5 is pretty standard, not pulling me in any particular direction, just a nice buzz. Grown outdoors organically in Northern California.

Sage 'N Sour

T.H.Seeds has gone and crossed the wicked-strong and tasty Sour Diesel (see *Cannabible 1*, page 163) with the legendary S.A.G.E. (see *Cannabible 1*, page 154) to create a hybrid of mind-boggling flavor and potency. Sage 'N Sour is an easy plant to grow, preferring large quantities of fertilizer. Finishing in around seventy days, she's quicker than the pure S.A.G.E. When all is said and done, the yield is higher than that of the pure Sour Diesel. Gotta love that hybrid vigor! The flavor of Sage 'N Sour is brilliant, complex, and unique. It's a bizarre combination of lemon candy and fuel, with other earthy and not-from-earth tones. The high is soaring and gave me little rushes up my spine after a giant fatty smoked to my head while in Amsterdam. Grown indoors organically in soil.

Sheherazade, the heroine of *The Arabian Nights*, is now also a cannabis strain thanks to Paradise Seeds. The heritage of Sheherazade is a bit mysterious. The mother is an Afghani plant that is said to have shown resin on the stem when only three inches tall. The father is a mystery sativa that was passed on to the breeders at Paradise several years ago. Expressions of both parents can clearly be seen, and choosing the right phenotype should be a breeze. I recommend the more sativa phenotype, as it will most likely have a more cerebral high. The flavor of Sheherazade is musky all the way, with sweet, floral, perfumey undertones. The high is relaxing and slightly euphoric. Sheherazade's yield is moderate to average depending on the phenotype chosen, and she harvests indoors in fifty-six to sixty days. Grown indoors hydroponically in Amsterdam.

Sheherazade

This monster is from the Shishkeberry line from Spice of Life Seeds. As for pedigree details, Shishkeberry was mothered by two Afghani hybrid cousins known as "the red" and "the yellow." The father was an especially resinous Blueberry (see *Cannabible 1*, page 44) from DJ Short's collection. The plants were selected for yield and resin production, respectively. The project was apparently a success, as Shishkeberry produces incredibly sparkly and resinous colas of seriously massive girth. The aroma of the live plant is intense, a combination of astringent, berry, hashy, and flowery scents. Unfortunately, the flavor of the finished product is not as desirable; it's more of a bland smoke. As I mentioned earlier, these plants were selected for yield and resin production, not flavor. But, whoa Nellie, do these things crank out the resin! I'm not sure I've ever seen a strain yield more sticky bubble hash per pull than Shishkeberry. Breeder Steve agrees with me on this one! There is a very early phenotype in the Shishkeberry line, and the strain is also known to do well when planted late in the season. Grown outdoors organically in Mendocino, California. Also pictured are Shishkeberry x Warlock, Shishkeberry x Big Blue, and Shishkeberry x Dutch Treat.

>>

Shishkeberry

Shoreline

Shoreline is a strain well-known in Texas. The story goes like this: Sometime in the late 1980s or early 1990s, some heads went to see the Grateful Dead at the Shoreline Amphitheater in California and scored a stinky sack of herb in the parking lot. In one nugget they found a seed, and this was brought home to Austin, Texas, where it was grown. The plant turned out quite nice, and clones of it are passed around Texas to this day. It seemed logical to the grower to name the strain after the venue at which it was scored. The lineage is unknown, but it seems to me to be an obvious Skunk selection. There is a pronounced skunky and hashy flavor, with a slight chocolate undertone and a suggestion of lemons. The yield of Shoreline is average at best, and the plant harvests indoors in around forty-five days. Watch out for the smell on this one—she's quite stinky!

The thick indica known as Afghooey (see *Cannabible 2*, page 9) was crossed with Sensi Seeds Silver Haze (*Cannabible 1*, page 158) to create this sexy hybrid. This cross is new to Northern California, and it looks like it's gonna be a keeper, as the massive yields of the Afghooey have been retained while the much more flavorful Silver Haze brings up the taste. Silver Goo is quite unstable, but both parents are of high quality so almost everything that comes up is worth keeping. I prefer the plants leaning toward the Silver Haze papa because they have a much more pronounced flavor, a spicy fruit combo that hits the spot every time. The phenotype closer to the Afghooey mother will be heavier yielding and a bit quicker, but the flavor is lacking, in my opinion. Silver Goo is strong medicine—a bit heavy for some but not a complete couchlock. The Haze influence brings an up edge that balances the high nicely. Indoor and outdoor versions are shown. The outdoor plants were grown organically in Mendocino, California, and harvested in late September. The finished product is earthy and skunky and has a spicy edge that's quite enticing. Also pictured is an outdoor organic nugget of a related strain called Triad, which is (Silver Haze x S 1 5) x Afghooey (see following page).

Silver Goo, aka Third Eye

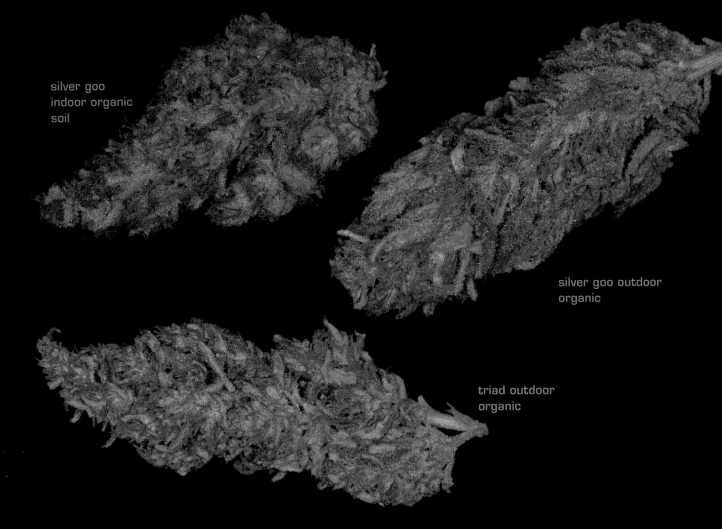

silver goo
indoor organic
soil

silver goo outdoor
organic

triad outdoor
organic

silver goo
indoor

This gorgeous specimen from Dutch Passion, called Skywalker, is a cross of Mazar (page 130) and DJ Short's Blueberry (see *Cannabible 1*, page 44). I like this strain, especially certain phenotypes that have a lovely fruity cola flavor with citrusy accentuations, an interesting and satisfying combination of flavors, to say the least. Skywalker gives a nice body stone, not quite couchlock (for me), but a nice thumpin' indica for sure. Indoors, she finishes in around sixty days. Outdoors, as pictured, harvest will be in early November. Grown outdoors in Mendocino, California.

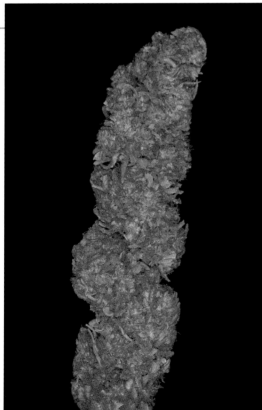

193

<< Snerval

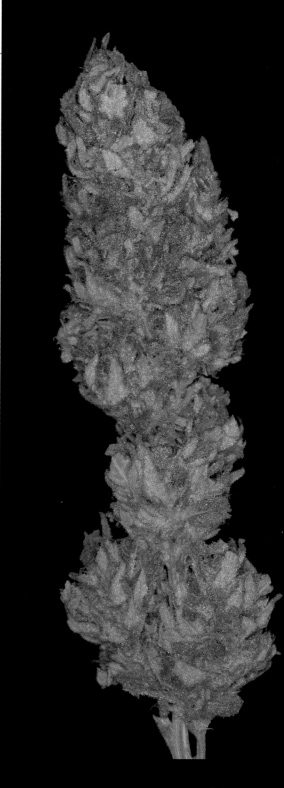

Snerval is simply some of the trippiest and most resinous herb I've ever had the pleasure of smoking. It comes from a mutant plant grown in the Columbia Gorge near Oregon's Mount Hood in 1993. The find was made by a skilled breeder with a great eye and nose for spotting rare and special qualities in a sea of plants. Seed stock is said to have originally come from Lopez Island, Washington. Clones were taken from this mutant, and the tips were then treated with gibberellic acid, causing a sex reversal from female to male. This provided a pollen source for making feminized seeds. Many generations later, the best of the best were then backcrossed with the original pollen, which had been kept frozen. This process was repeated seven times over two years to lock in and stabilize the desired traits, making Snerval a true F6.

Why go through all this? For one thing, the original plant showed trichomes on the stem and on the first set of leaves to open above the cotyledons (the plant's first set of leaves), and on all subsequent stems as well. Trichomes alone don't indicate potency or quality of high; a sample is necessary for that. Fortunately, the sample proved to be exceptional and worthy of this work. The aroma of Snerval is intense . . . and bizarre. It has an intense high note something like a pungent lemon-lime fabric softener and another tone that's similar to passion fruit, and it's rounded out by a thick, fruity Afghani bottom end—though not a fruit that exists on this planet. Other weird indescribable tones are in there as well. As for the high, well, let me tell you that being Snervalized is a very powerful experience. This herb is a great mind expander, helping one to achieve deep and broad insight while lying plastered on the kitchen floor, only to eventually eat every single thing in the refrigerator (great appetite stimulator!). Soon after, a deep restorative sleep is inevitable. Yes, it's extremely strong. Another interesting thing about Snerval is its unique propensity to grow J-shaped resin glands. Also noteworthy is that it grows several different kinds of glands: clusters of thousands of small dark amber glands with long stalks, giant red glands, and clusters of fat clear glands on short stalks. I've never seen another strain do this. It literally oozes resin. Grown outdoors organically in Santa Cruz, California. My compliments to the breeder and grower.

indoor with
powdery mildew

Snowcap is another of the highly distributed clones in the Bay Area medical cannabis clubs. I've heard several different stories on the lineage, but the most believable is that is was selected from the Sensi Seeds Indoor Mix. When grown indoors, **Snowcap** had poor resistance to powdery mildew, as you can see, rendering the finished product questionable, but it was still sold as medicine in a popular Bay Area club. The flavor from **Snowcap** is actually quite good, assuming you can find some that isn't moldy. It's candy sweet and almost tropical, with a touch of spice in the background. The high is balanced nicely in its effects, conversational but also with a nice solid buzz. Three different samples are shown: indoor hydro, Humboldt greenhouse, and Mendocino outdoor.

Snowcap

From the man who brought us HP13 comes his newest creation, **Sour P.** This feminized cross of arguably the two tastiest strains on the planet, HP13 (see *Cannabible 1*, page 75) and Sour Diesel (see *Cannabible 1*, page 163), is, as could be expected, insanely flavorful. Brilliant flavors from both mamas can be distinguished melding together on the palate, everything from intense salty skunk to sour tangy fuel. It's one of those strains that you'll never forget if you ever get to try it. The high from **Sour P** is extremely medicinal and does the trick every time, regardless of one's tolerance. It's euphoric and almost numbing at times, and a couple of tokes is all that most people need. Too bad it tastes so damned great that the puffing seems to go on until there's none left, regardless of the fact that people are almost tripping after two or three tokes! Unfortunately, the plants are hermaphroditic, due to the feminization process, and will be released only to a few. In the meantime, the breeder is doing the work needed to make Sour P a hermaphrodite-free reality. Pictured are indoor hydro-grown samples and an outdoor Maui version.

Sour P >>

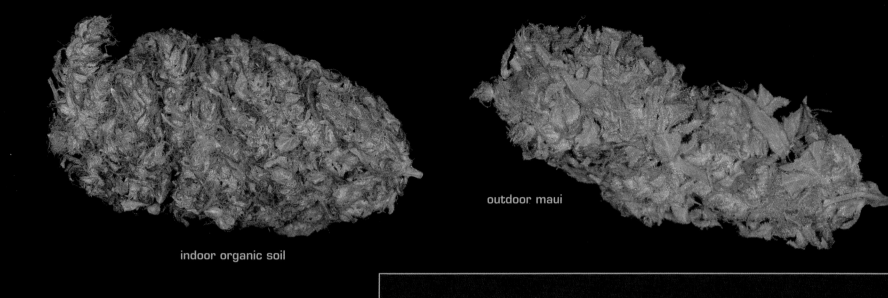
indoor organic soil

outdoor maui

hydro

hydro

197

Space
Queen

No longer available, Space Queen was a hybrid of Cindy 99 (see *Cannabible 2,* page 36) and Romulan (see *Cannabible 1*, page 57) from BCGA. (Can't come up with something new? Cross two strains that other people made!) You really can't go wrong with parents of this quality, though. The flavor from Space Queen is outstanding. It's like a mix of mentholated semirotten lemons with a hint of gasoline and pine trees. This might not sound too appealing to some, but trust me, this stuff tastes great. The plant grows somewhat wispy flowers, produces slightly lower-than-average yields, and finishes in around sixty days if you find the right phenotype. Apparently the "breeder" didn't do the work to stabilize this line, as the grower of these beautiful flowers found only one keeper in an entire pack of seeds. As for the high, this is really euphoric and giggly herb, and quite potent as well. It gave me uncontrollable munchies, too. Expertly grown indoors, mostly organically, in soil in the Midwest.

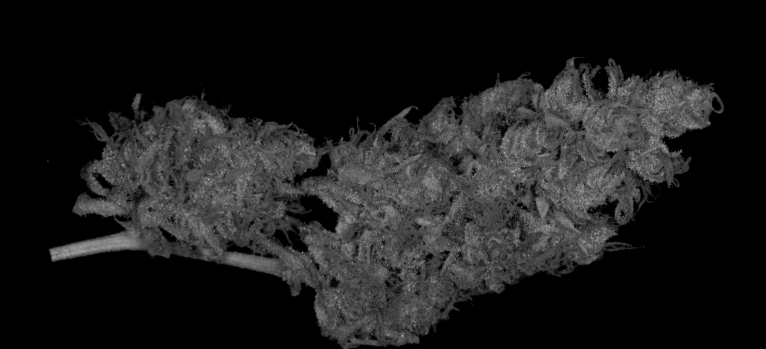

Another somewhat mysterious strain from Barney's Farm in Amsterdam, Stella Blue was available at Any Day Coffeeshop even before Barney's had it. The way I look at it, any strain named after such a great song must be great! Stella Blue has an earthy, rich flavor suggesting fresh blueberries. The smoke is incredibly smooth and satisfying, though not overwhelmingly flavorful. Following is a crisp head high that would surely please any connoisseur. It's been reported that seeds of Stella Blue crosses will be made available.

Stella Blue

200

Strawberry
<< Cough

This legendary East Coast strain was created by crossing Strawberry Fields, a pure indica from Vermont, with a pure Haze male. It is reported that the original Strawberry Fields is now extinct. One particular clone of Strawberry Cough is the main one going around these days, and that's what I review here. This particular clone is a very heavy yielder of glowing, bright, rotund red nuggets with a lovely strawberry'n'spice flavor. The plants prefer a low fertilization program and take about nine weeks to flower. The high is nicely balanced, cerebral but also euphoric and not lacking body. Dutch Passion has recently released a hybrid of Strawberry Cough. It's unclear what they crossed it with, but the samples I've seen don't much resemble the pure Strawberry Cough. Grown indoors organically in soil by Kyle Kushman, the breeder himself!

From Homegrown Fantaseeds in Amsterdam we have Super Crystal, which they call a "Shiva mix." This short and squat mostly indica strain takes around fifty-five days to harvest indoors. According to growers who have raised it, it has a flavor ranging from oriental spice to burning tires, depending on which phenotype is chosen. Good luck.

Super Crystal

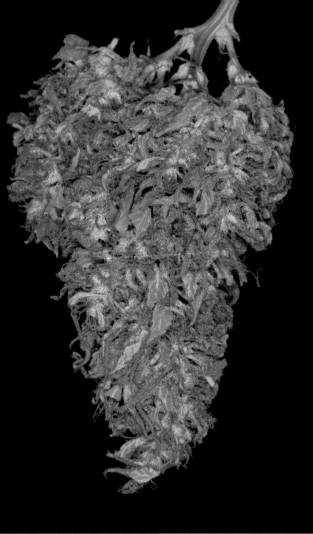

<< Swazi

From the tiny landlocked southeastern African nation of Swaziland comes the landrace sativa known as Swazi. Swaziland is the biggest producer of dagga (an African word for marijuana) in Africa. Swazi can be scored at various places throughout Africa, and the quality varies greatly. Most of the people I speak to who live in Africa agree that the Swazi going around has gone downhill in recent years. Still, there are occasional fantastic batches that come around. The plants usually put out long sticky buds with earthy flavors ranging from licorice to pine. This sativa gives a very up high felt almost completely in the head. The plants are very early for a sativa, finishing indoors in as little as fifty-five days, and outdoors in late September. This sample was grown from pure Swazi seed stock in Mendocino, California. Look for Africa-grown Swazi in a future Cannabible, as the seasons permit.

Sweet Tart >>

These lovely ladies are a creation of a breeder named Rain Man, who's based in Northern California. A stunning Kush plant was crossed with a particularly luscious mystery sativa to make this hybrid. Two main phenotypes are shown: one leaning toward the Kush and one leaning toward the sativa. Both are excellent. The flavor of Sweet Tart is just that, sweet and tart, with heavy syrup overtones. It's an extremely smooth and satisfying smoke, tasty down to the last toke. The high from Sweet Tart is wonderful, extremely mellow and meditative, with a thick head effect—a perfect smoke for relaxing after a long day. These plants were grown outdoors organically in Humboldt, California.

sativa phenotype

indica phenotype

sativa
phenotype

indica
phenotype

203

Taskenti

Hailing from a Spanish company known as Canna Biogen, Taskenti is a pure landrace indica that originated in Uzbekistan, home to some of the finest hashish in the world. This herb has an interesting flavor, a light combination of hash, menthol, and mint, with hints of lemon. When grown indoors, the flowering time is approximately seven to nine weeks. Outdoors, expect harvest in mid-October. When flowering, the plants prefer a dry atmosphere with good ventilation. The high from Taskenti is quite up for an indica, though if you smoke too much you'll probably be horizontal within an hour. Grown in an inland greenhouse in Humboldt, California.

Two exotic landrace sativas meet in this sativa lover's dream. These nugs were grown from seed in British Columbia, and there was lots of variety present. Good luck finding a bud that isn't unique and delicious in this fine herb! Some of the buds leaned more toward the Thai, evident by the classic Thai flavor, which is something like an earthy light tobacco, for lack of a better word, often with hints of citrus and anise. Others lean toward the Nepali, which has a more fruity and floral flavor, sometimes with hashy undertones. The high from this herb is cerebral and heady all the way, great for deep spiritual conversations or making music. It is a real treat to smoke landrace sativas that were dried, cured, and handled properly. The export product (whatever is still exported, which is not much) from third world countries such as these is normally dried too fast and with too much light present, cured improperly if at all, and smashed to oblivion before being smuggled. The quality suffers greatly as a result. Grown outdoors organically in Vancouver.

Thai x Nepali

FIM TECHNIQUE

There is a new and accidentally discovered pruning method known as FIM, which, believe it or not, stands for "Fuck, I missed!" FIMming is similar to topping, but instead of cutting the main stem, the plant is given what seems like a tight haircut. The cutter removes 25 to 75 percent of the leaves shooting from the top of the plant or branch. The best time to FIM is when the plant is at its fifth node. The vegetation that is left behind has cells that are dividing rapidly, leading to multiple tops from a single pruning. The cool thing about FIMming is that you don't lose the main cola, as with traditional topping. Instead of getting the two tops that result from traditional topping, you can get as many as eight. What's happening is that the top of the plant is temporarily stunted, and as it heals, the side branches continue growing, perhaps even experiencing an accelerated growth phase. What you end up with is a plant with multiple main colas instead of one. This is highly beneficial to indoor growers trying to maximize the amount of light reaching the flowers. This technique works great with indicas, but it can be more challenging with sativas due to their lanky structure.

Skeptics of the FIM technique point out that since the commercial fruit and flower industries don't use the technique, it must be pointless. I disagree with this theory. For one thing, many "professional" techniques used today were discovered by amateurs, and often by accident. Simply because FIM hasn't caught on in the commercial industries means nothing. Additionally, if these "pros" understood plants so well, they wouldn't be drowning them in chemicals day after day. Clearly, more research is needed on this subject. I'd like to see experiments done in which clones are taken of a single strain and grown in identical conditions, but some would be left to grow naturally, some would be topped, and some would be FIMmed. At the end, the dried buds from each plant would be weighed. I mean, this *is* all about yield, right?

A note on pruning: I often see growers removing large fan leaves, thinking this will let more light in to the flowers and increase production. This is simply not true—in fact, quite the opposite is true. Mother Nature doesn't make mistakes, and she put those large leaves there for a reason. Think of the fan leaves as photosynthesis factories, taking in all that light and converting it into the sugars and other foods necessary for bud production. When you remove these leaves, you're reducing the plant's ability to photosynthesize and therefore reducing its output of flowers. Removing large fan leaves also screws with the plant's metabolism, which can have all sorts of negative effects, including sex reversal. When the plant is finished with a leaf, it will let it go naturally, after removing all stored food reserves. If a gentle tug on a leaf does not release it, "leave" it alone is my advice.

<< cut here

Trance

In an effort to make an earlier-harvesting Skunk strain for outdoor applications, Dutch Passion crossed in an early indica strain and released these F1 seeds as Trance. Tested at 11.1 percent THC, Trance has a mild skunky and fruity flavor—nothing overly exciting, but decent. If you want an early harvesting outdoor Skunk, this could be the one for you. Grown outdoors in Northern California.

Reeferman crossed three different heir-loom Afghanis together to create the Triple Afghan Slam (TAS), which I photographed (in the rain) while visiting him in Canada. These plants are hardy, resistant to mold, and finish quickly, making TAS a suitable outdoor strain for northern climates. This strain is indica all the way, growing about six feet tall, with fat and broad-bladed leaves, and producing chunky fluorescent green nugs with a hashy and pungent aroma and flavor. The high is sedative, relaxing, and thick. Also of interest is that this is a low-odor strain, another major benefit for many clandestine growers. The plants finish in mid- to late September outdoors, while indoors, where they are also suitable, they finish in seven to eight weeks.

Triple Afghan Slam

A remake of the classic Blueberry, True Blueberry, unlike the original, was selected from a very large pool, and some great selections were made indeed. True Blueberry has everything we all loved about the original Blueberry, but better. The flavor is the best part, and let me tell you, these nugs really taste like blueberries. This, of course, is even more mind-boggling considering the herb actually grows with intense blue colorings. (Did Mother Nature do that, or DJ Short?) When grown indoors, in seven to eight weeks True Blueberry produces above-average yields of connoisseur-quality herb sure to please even a pot snob like myself. The high from True Blueberry is high indeed, though completely functionable. This is great daytime herb. It's not lacking in potency at all, it's just not devastating like so many indicas can be. Masterfully grown indoors organically in a hydroponic garden.

True Blueberry >>

<< Twilight

Twilight, from Dutch Passion, is a gorgeously colorful indica strain. Though it's listed as an outdoor strain, people have reported having good luck with it indoors as well. These are some of the lower-priced seeds from Dutch Passion, and I must say, given the price I was rather impressed with the strain. For an indica, Twilight really stretches out, so please be aware of that if you choose to grow it, especially indoors. The flavor from Twilight is hard to describe. It's like slightly rotten fruit, but in a good way, if that's possible. Not my favorite flavor ever, but not bad either. The high, though not overly strong, is thick and heavy, encouraging the horizontalization of the rest of my night. With a flowering time of fifty to fifty-five days, high yields, and a beautiful purple finished product, Twilight should be a welcome addition to any indica lover's garden. Pictured are two different outdoor batches from California: one grown in Fort Bragg, the other in Mendocino.

Ultra Skunk

In an experiment in Switzerland, Dutch Passion Seeds flowered a large selection of different Dutch and Swiss Skunk seeds and clones to select the best possible Skunk. When the best two Skunks were identified, they were crossed and the Ultra Skunk was born. The flavor is sweet and soft, not really skunky, at least in comparison to American Skunk. This is typical of Dutch Skunks. It seems that most Dutch breeders tend to select for sweet plants. The high from Ultra Skunk is also typical Skunk, mostly felt in the head but with a soft and mellow body buzz as well. Grown outdoors in Northern California.

goshen goop

VERMONT

On a trip to Vermont to see Coventry, the final Phish shows, I shot these beautiful nugs. Make no mistake about it—there are killer nugs in Vermont! Many choices of awesome indoor ganja were available, as well as local outdoor strains—early harvesting indicas that are fast enough to beat the first frost. Due to Vermont's close proximity to Canada, there was plenty of Beasters around as well (low-quality mass-produced Canadian schwag). There are many serious herb aficionados in these parts, as well as unique local strains like this "Goshen Goop." Thanks for the shows, boys!

goshen goop

212

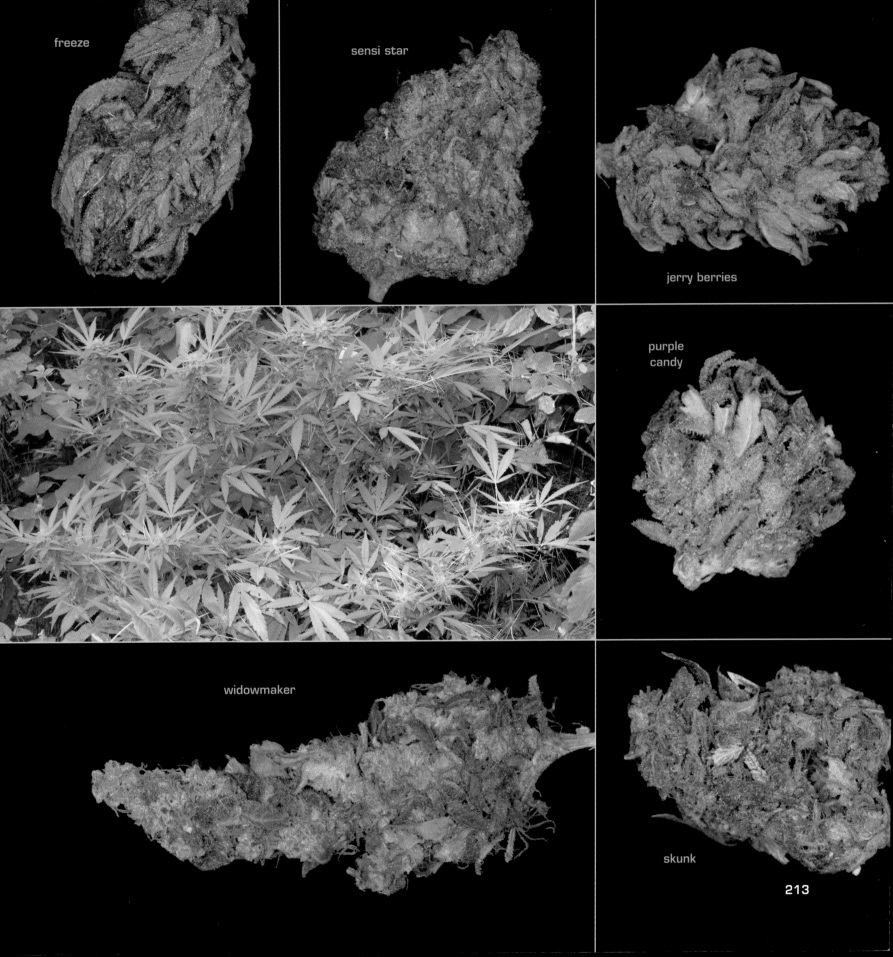

freeze

sensi star

jerry berries

purple
candy

widowmaker

skunk

213

GENETICALLY MODIFIED CANNABIS

BY CHIMERA

The genetic modification of food and flower crops is common practice these days; if you live in North America and eat any processed or mass-produced food, it's likely that you're eating an ingredient that has been subjected to genetic modification. Corn, soy, potatoes, rice, sugar beets, wheat, flax, and even radicchio have been subjected to genetic engineering to improve each crop's respective growth characteristics or nutritional values. This has become a topic of concern among consumers who are unsure of the possible consequences of genetically modified plants on human health, as well as on the ecological balance of the environment.

I often ask cultivators if they would grow genetically modified (GM) marijuana; for most, the initial answer is, "No way, absolutely not." I then ask them if they would like to grow their favorite cultivar or clone outside and have it be completely resistant to *Botrytis cinerea* (gray mold, a blight that affects vast numbers of plants every year and reduces the yield for growers worldwide). Most think about it for a second and then respond, "Wow, you can do that? You mean my plants would never mold again? That is definitely something I'd be willing to look into."

What exactly is genetic modification, or genetic engineering? Genetic modification is the process of transferring a gene from one individual or species to a new individual or species without using conventional pollination techniques. Through various technologies, a new gene (the transgene) is actually inserted and incorporated into the genetic blueprint of the target host individual, where it will reside in every cell of the plant and be passed on to future generations. The inserted gene of interest is expressed in the new host individual, which confers the function of that particular gene to the new host. (In the example above, the new gene is responsible for the resistance to the gray mold.)

Manipulating genes on this level is not a simple task, and each species presents unique obstacles that researchers must overcome before successful genetic transformations can take place. These obstacles have now been overcome with respect to cannabis. A research group in Europe has successfully transferred a gene from a species of bacteria into the genome of a hemp variety. This allows the GM plants to substantially resist the devastating fungal infection known as gray mold, while non-GM plants grown alongside are literally destroyed by the mold. *Botrytis cinerea* can simply not grow in the presence of the gene product.

You may have heard a rumor that spread around the Internet a few years ago claiming that someone had created a variety of tomato that produced THC. Although this rumor was categorically untrue, the possibility of using other plants as "bioreactors" for THC is entirely possible. In 2004, a Japanese research team successfully transferred a gene from cannabis into tobacco. The gene was involved in the THC-synthesis pathway, and when specific precursors were fed to the tobacco plant via its roots, it converted the precursors into THC. This was the first time in history that THC had been found in any species other than cannabis.

One can see from the above examples that GM technologies have great potential for crop production. Now that it's possible to modify cannabis at the genetic level, the possibilities are tremendous: Plants could be created to produce higher levels of THC than occur naturally, to resist pests and diseases, or to be sexually sterile. Imagine being able to cultivate a sterile drug plant in the middle of a hemp field and have it remain completely seed free.

Many are against GM technologies; some because they want to be able to choose whether they consume GM products or not (current regulations don't adequately address this issue), and some because they believe these transgenes can spread through natural or cultivated populations unbeknownst to the grower or consumer. And indeed, researchers have already found nonspecies transgenes present in the wild or in undomesticated ancestors of corn. Because cannabis is wind pollinated, if steps aren't taken to confine the transgenes to the varieties to which they were introduced, it's inevitable that we'll find them in populations they were never intended to be in.

Cannabis is illegal in most places on earth, and as such the trade in cannabis seeds, clones, and flowers is not regulated, as it is for legal plants. Most of the trade in these products is in black market situations. Legal GM crops must be approved for use to ensure they are tested for health safety and to prevent transgenes from spreading to locally cultivated varieties. There is no practical way to ensure that the buds in your bag are GM free. Although the potential of GM cannabis is exciting for some, those who wish to embark on the path of this type of research must keep in mind that their present actions may have unintended future consequences, and all responsible researchers should make every effort to ensure that the transgenic modifications they undertake today don't have a negative impact on our beloved plant in the future.

JK's Note: For the record, I am strongly against the genetic modification of cannabis or any of God's creations, for that matter, but I feel it is appropriate to include this information as food for thought. In my view, skilled breeders can create a strain that's resistant to mold or one that pumps out copious amounts of resin, if that's what's desired. Want something even stronger? Make some hash! There is simply no need to screw around with the genes of a plant when we really have no idea of the future implications of this process.

The only reason companies like Monsanto do it is because you can't patent a plant, but you certainly can patent a GM plant. This way, everyone has to buy it from them! All the while, they claim that they're doing this to help feed the starving masses of the world. What a crock! And if that wasn't bad enough, when non-GM farmers, even those who are totally against GM, experience the nightmare of having their crops contaminated by GM products, they are sued by these evil corporations for royalties on their patents!

Additionally, as Chimera mentioned, because cannabis is a wind-pollinated species, it's inevitable that these "Frankenpot" genes will make their way into the regular cannabis gene pool, never to be removed. We must make sure this never happens. As one example of the unforeseen effects of GM crops, consider that in one study researchers dusted GM maize pollen onto the leaves of milkweed, commonly found on the edges of cornfields, and also the main source of food for Monarch butterflies. Half the Monarch butterflies died, and the rest grew to only 50 percent of normal size. Personally, I go to great lengths to avoid eating anything that's GM, meaning I almost never eat in restaurants, I grow as much of my own food as possible, and I buy food only at natural food stores (and even then you can't be sure). It sucks to have to be so vigilant, but this is the way it is with our current "food" supply.

If you're thinking that cannabis lovers don't have to worry too much about genetic engineering, consider these facts: The U.S. government under Clinton spent $23 million to design a GM fungus that could destroy ganja and coca plants. Known as *Fusarium oxysporum* EN4, this fungus is not host specific, meaning that it could not only be devastating for ganja plants, it could also spell disaster for entire ecosystems. On their patent applications for the "Terminator" gene, which prevents plants from producing fertile seeds (so farmers have to buy new seeds each year), Monsanto lists cannabis/hemp as one of the plants for which the technology is effective—just in case it's ever legalized.

tom hill

reeferman

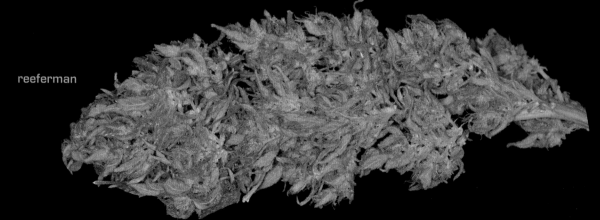

Vietnamese Black

Here we have a wicked landrace sativa from Vietnam. While the flavor is nothing special, the high is very special indeed. It's very different from the indica-based strains most of us smoke today. It doesn't seem very strong at first, but soon after a couple of tokes, a heart-racing and soaring high envelops your very existence. It's too speedy for some, and some people even break out in sweats from smoking it. The flowering time is predictably very long on this lanky sativa, preferably at least sixteen weeks. But once the wait is over, you can count on some unique and stratospherically stony herb. Pictured are two versions, one from the Reeferman, grown outdoors in Vancouver, and another from a breeder named Tom Hill, grown in a greenhouse in Mendocino, California.

tom hill

reeferman

Voodoo

Yet another from the extensive line of Dutch Passion offerings, Voodoo is a trippy sativa originating in Thailand but worked over thoroughly by the breeders at Dutch Passion. The plant produces long, thick buds with a complex flavor ranging from fruity to spicy to musky, with other weird undertones, including anise. Voodoo is surprisingly compact for a Thai, no doubt the selecting skills of Dutch Passion coming in to play here. The high from Voodoo is heady and crisp, a nice treat for a sativa lover such as myself. It was tested at 8.2 percent THC and less than 0.1 percent cannabidiol, so you can see that it isn't insanely potent, but it's a great daytime smoke in my opinion. Expect moderate yields from this one; she's more of a heady strain than a commercial producer. Grown outdoors in Mendocino, California.

From Valchanvre Seeds in Switzerland we have Walliser Queen, winner of the Canna Swiss Cup in 1998. Hemp Queen might be a more appropriate name. This herb had very little flavor and no noticeable high (with my tolerance, anyway). I'd like to hope or imagine the batch that won the Canna Swiss Cup was better. Please, unless you live in a very cold climate where nothing else will grow, do not grow this stuff. Walliser Queen is surely a ruderalis strain, known for early flowering and ultralow THC. Grown outdoors in Mendocino, California. Interesting note: Bernard Rappaz, the breeder of Walliser Queen, was busted with, get this, fifty-two thousand kilos (the amount needed to get high from this shit?) and a ton of hash. The industrious man is now free after a hunger strike in prison.

Walliser Queen

outdoor
organic

hydro

220

<< Werthers

What do you get when you cross the legendary and highly sought-after HP13 with an amazing old-school Oaxacan sativa? Pure bliss, people. Peee-ure bliss. It is often nearly impossible to describe the flavors and aromas of fine ganja, because those flavors and aromas exist nowhere else in nature, so there literally are no words that fit. This luscious strain, on the other hand, can be described exactly. It smells and luckily tastes identical to Werthers butterscotch candy, mixed in a blender with a rum and coke, and some Juicy Fruit gum. This exotic cross is definitely leaning toward the Oaxacan side of the equation, though the wickedly strong flavor of the HP13 comes brilliantly shining through as well. The high from this exotic herb is also extremely desirable—powerful yet extremely "up," perfect for an inspirational morning joint.

Willie Nelson >>

I can pretty much guarantee that if you love sativas, you will love Willie. Bred by Reeferman specifically for the man himself, a devout sativa lover, Willie Nelson (the strain) is a hybrid of Vietnamese Black (page 217) and a sativa from the Nepalese highlands. The flavor, as you might have guessed, is quite exotic. Sour, sweet, and lemony smoke was quickly followed by a borderline psychedelic high—soaring cerebral sativa goodness in all its glory. This is happy herb, or maybe I was happy because it tasted so good, but either way, yum! Willie takes ten weeks to flower indoors and, given the right conditions, can be a good yielder as well. Outdoors, expect Willie to finish in mid- to late October, quite early for a sativa. This strain, sold at Barney's Breakfast Bar, deservingly won the Cannabis Cup in 2005. Grown indoors organically in soil.

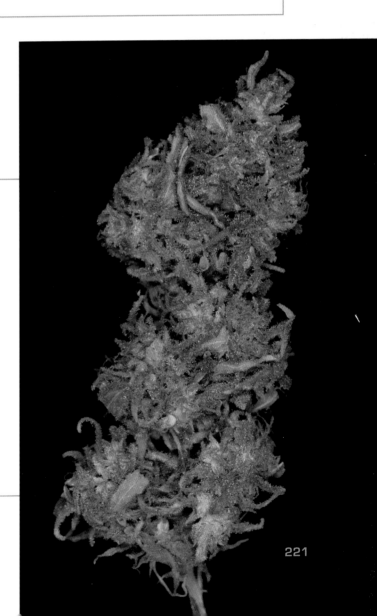

Errata to CANNABIBLES 1 and 2

CANNABIBLE 1

Page 32: Asian Fantasy—one phenotype is still alive. She is difficult to grow and really wants to be outside.

Page 35: This bud is 50 percent Big Bud and would have been a lot better if it was grown better.

Page 41: Blaze is Blueberry x Haze.

Page 52: California Sativa should not have been included.

Page 54: BC outdoor should not have been included—lack of information.

Page 56: Iggy should not have been included—lack of information.

Page 58: Cat Piss is a clone-only strain mostly seen on the West Coast.

Page 61: Cristallica—no longer offered.

Page 63: Desert Outdoor Organic should not have been included—lack of information.

Page 65: Doc Kevorkian—this one probably would be great if grown well. This sample was not.

Page 72: Gak should not have been included—lack of information.

Page 72: Great White Shark—would have been much better if grown organically. Now sold as Shark Shock from Mr Nice Seeds.

Page 75: HP13 genetics are now better understood. This is a pure Afghani with some Thai genetics mixed in.

Page 133: Molasses should not have been included—lack of information.

Page 135: Mt. Shasta should not have been included—lack of information.

Page 145: Palm Springs Outdoor should not have been included—lack of information.

Page 166: Stretch—should not have been included—not an actual strain.

Page 177: Top 44—I have since smoked Top 44 that was grown expertly, and it was actually pretty good!

Page 179: Warlock is from Magus Genetics.

CANNABIBLE 2

Page 12: Brothers Grimm is now out of business, but there are several other companies selling Apollo hybrids.

Page 46: I have since smoked organic Dawg that was as good as any chemmy Chem.

Page 47: Coastal Gold should not have been included—lack of information.

Page 49: Coral Reef is Hawaiian Sativa x Bubbleberry.

Page 53: These are all Diesel hybrids that a grower in North Carolina was working with. They should not have been included—lack of information.

Page 62: Dynamite seeds are available from Next Generation Seeds.

Page 75: Hasan should not have been included—lack of information.

Page 79: Island Sweet Skunk—Federation—stolen genetics from Spice of Life Seeds.

Page 80: Jack Candy should not have been included; it's included just as an F2 of Jack Flash.

Page 91: L.A. Rose should not have been included—lack of information.

Page 109: Morning Star should not have been included—lack of information.

Page 110: When grown outdoors, Mothership is not as flavorful and has more of a coffee/chocolate flavor. Definitely not a HP13-Diesel cross, this one is a pure sativa (and very mold resistant).

Page 118: Ninja should not have been included—lack of information.

Page 120: Omega should not have been included—lack of information.

Page 137: Salmon Creek Big Bud is a Sensi Seeds Big Bud selection (meaning 50 percent Big Bud, 50 percent Skunk).

Page 148: Stone Blue should not have been included—lack of information.

Recommended Reading

The *Paradigm* series from Bridger House Publishers, and all books recommended within the series.